Unbridled Resilience: Women in Running

Tales of Determination, Courage, and Passion for the Run, Harnessing Strength One Stride at a Time, and Meeting the Distinct Needs of Today's Female Athlete

Sarah Russell

Table of Contents

Introduction

Women today lead busy lives, juggling child care, work, education, social life, and self-care. Adding long-distance running to the equation—or even thinking about it—can be very overwhelming. Yet, despite these obligations, many women are finding ways to balance responsibilities, carving out space for long-distance running.

If you have been looking for ways to improve your life, I am excited to tell you that running is your superpower, your best self-help manual to enhance your life! As a passionate runner, running has been a critical part of my lifestyle, positively impacting my life.

Running has been part of me, and I am convinced that running is a woman's superpower. Running, especially long-distance races, has allowed women to shatter barriers and blaze trails for decades. That is the reason I draw strength from inspiring stories of prominent women like the 60-year-old Kate Dunbar, who, despite her diagnosis of psoriatic arthritis at the age of 40, arguably broke a record of running a marathon and a half-marathon in the space of two weeks. This feat is far from many people's perception of possibility.

When interviewed, she said (Walsh, 2023):

> I'm feeling absolutely fine, totally recovered. I did track training as well during the middle of the week. Apparently, you're not supposed to run much in the days after a marathon, but that's the power of my diet; it's so anti-inflammatory that you heal quickly. (para. 3)

Undoubtedly, Kate understands that the motivation behind being a great runner spans from a mix of different healthy habits and lifestyles adopted intentionally. I have been running for over 15 years, but the last 6 years have narrowed my passion to trail running and ultramarathons. Running has helped me to find myself and learn who I am. It has given me so much freedom from anxiety and depression. So, I would say that self-discovery and emotional closure are the essential blessings running has offered me. Other women have something similar or even more empowering in it for them.

A short while ago, I was casually discussing the evolution of running over time and the inclusiveness of women. I listened to a few fellow runners who were not just women but ones who understood the dynamics of running as a woman and were not reserved about sharing their histories, stories, and bits of experience. I also considered the hurdles we face as sportswomen whose anatomy and physiology differ from men's, from our ever-fluctuating hormones to menstruation and pregnancy. This is even more challenging for women in more tasking running niches like long-distance races and marathons.

The history of women's long-distance running is a remarkable journey from exclusion to pronounced visibility. Formerly, societal norms and medical misconceptions opined that women were physically unfit for endurance sports. The early 20th century opened up a few opportunities for women in competitive long-distance running.

The paradigm shift began in the mid-20th century, prompted by the early women who sat out these norms. In 1966, Roberta "Bobbi" Gibb became the first woman to run the Boston Marathon unofficially, followed by Kathrine Switzer in 1967, who famously registered under a gender-neutral name and completed the race despite several attempts to remove her from this course.

There were subsequent significant turning points in the following years, and women's long-distance running has flourished. Today, women's long-distance running is celebrated globally, with women participating in marathons, ultramarathons, and other endurance events at all levels, showcasing their strength and resilience.

This book will teach you about other inspiring women who made giant strides. You will learn about Stamata Revithi, a woman whose story inspires me in many significant ways. Although women were prohibited from participation, Stamata Revithi defied all odds and insisted on running the 40-kilometer marathon during the 1896 Summer Olympics. Her daring move paved the way for more resilience from women afterward.

You will meet other women from all walks of life, each with their unique struggles and triumphs. From battling societal constraints to overcoming personal setbacks, each woman embodies the spirit of unbridled resilience. These women have found solace, strength, and identity in running. Their stories are diverse yet interconnected by a common thread of resilience. Their journeys highlight today's female athletes' distinct needs and experiences, shedding light on the intricate balance between physical training, mental fortitude, and emotional well-being.

However, here is a caution: *Women in Running* is not merely a collection of stories but a chronicle of the strength and spirit that characterize female runners worldwide. From the seasoned marathoner to the novice jogger, each category encapsulates the essence of resilience, highlighting women's unique challenges and triumphs in running. As you enjoy the stories, endeavor to pick the lessons therein.

Running has always been more than a physical endeavor. It is a journey of mental fortitude and emotional growth. For women, it often signifies breaking free from societal expectations, embracing one's identity, and pursuing personal goals with unwavering resolve. This book seeks to honor your journey, offering a glimpse into the lives of female runners who inspire us with their stories of perseverance and triumph.

While we navigate through their experiences, we will also explore the evolving landscape of women's sports, the distinct needs of today's female athletes, the importance of community and support, and the necessity of advocating for equality and recognition. Through expert insights and personal anecdotes, I am providing you valuable insights on training the ever-important balance between competition and self-care.

As you embark on this journey, you will find inspiration and empowerment from this. No matter your level as a female runner, you will be equipped with knowledge, stories, and advice that resonate with your experiences and aspirations.

Chapter 1:

The Unstoppable Spirit

All you need is the courage to believe in yourself and put one foot in front of the other. —Kathrine Switzer

A phenomenon exists in the realm of runners that transcends beyond mere physicality. This phenomenon is aptly called *"The Unstoppable Spirit."* It is the heartbeat of the sprinting journey, the driving force behind every bold stride, and the beam that guides us through challenges and triumphs. This unstoppable spirit was what Kathrine Switzer was referring to as "the courage to believe in yourself."

Kathrine Switzer's timeless wisdom sets the stage for exploring other inspiring female runners who have been remarkably outstanding in the running world. A woman like her is worth exploring. Thus, this chapter will examine her inspiring life, relentless determination, and unwavering passion.

Who Is Kathrine Switzer?

Kathrine Switzer's journey as a pioneer in women's running is proof of her resilience, determination, and commitment to breaking barriers. Born on January 5, 1947, in Amberg, Germany, Switzer's path to becoming a trailblazer in athletics was not so smooth.

Switzer was introduced to running during her teenage years. She attended Lynchburg College in Virginia on a track scholarship and continued pursuing her love for running after moving to Syracuse. However, her decision to enter the Boston Marathon in 1967 catapulted her into the spotlight and forever changed the landscape of women's running.

At the time, the Boston Marathon was a prestigious event reserved exclusively for male participants. Women were not considered capable of enduring the grueling 42.2-kilometer race. No provisions were made for female entrants. Unbothered by the prevailing limitations and exclusions towards women in sports, Switzer registered for the marathon under the unisex name "K.V. Switzer."

On April 19, 1967, Switzer treaded the starting line of the Boston Marathon along with her male counterparts. There was skepticism and resistance from some of the male runners and officials, but she wasn't moved. Moved by mere personal determination, she embarked on her historic course, oblivious of her participation's groundbreaking impact on future generations.

Several miles into the race, a race official, Jock Semple, reportedly attempted to remove Switzer from the race upon realizing she was a woman. However, a few of Switzer's male companions supported her audacity and shielded her from Semple's grasp, allowing her to continue running. Switzer finished the Boston Marathon in approximately 4 hours and 20 minutes.

In the face of adversity, Switzer's staunchness caught the media's attention and sparked a global conversation and controversy about gender equality in sports. Her determination to challenge the status quo and prove that women could compete in endurance events earned her widespread admiration and respect.

After her groundbreaking run at the Boston Marathon, Switzer dedicated herself to advocating for women's participation in sports and promoting gender equality. She became a spokesperson for the women's running movement and traveled worldwide to inspire and empower women to pursue their athletic dreams. Switzer's efforts played a salient role in breaking down barriers and creating new opportunities for female athletes in traditionally male-dominated sports.

In addition to her advocacy work, Switzer continued to excel as a competitive runner by achieving several accolades throughout her career. After winning the New York City Marathon in 1974, with a time of 3:07:29 (59th overall), she went on to compete in the Olympic Games in 1972. Her achievements in running further qualified her as a trailblazer and role model for generations of female athletes.

Switzer was named Female Runner of the Decade (1967–77) by Runner's World Magazine and was equally inducted into the National Women's Hall of Fame in 2011 in recognition of her contributions to the advancement of women in sports. Her resilient spirit and unwavering commitment to equality inspire countless individuals worldwide to defy expectations and pursue their passions on and off the track.

Kathrine Switzer faced numerous challenges while attempting to break the status quo. Here are a few of them:

- **Dealing with systemic sexism:** Just like many other sports at the time, The Boston Marathon had some strict gender-based rules that prevented women from participating. Switzer encountered entrenched sexism within the sporting community, where women were often dismissed as unfit to compete in endurance events like marathons. Among several other misconceptions, it was believed a woman's uterus could fall out during such sports.

- **Official resistance:** After registering for the marathon under the gender-neutral name "K.V. Switzer," race officials initially accepted her application without realizing she was a woman. An official attempted to remove her from the race when Switzer appeared on the course. This is a testament to the pervasive attitudes towards women in sports.

- **Media scrutiny:** Switzer's participation in the Boston Marathon garnered significant media attention, pushing her into the spotlight and subjecting her to intense scrutiny. While some coverages were supportive, others' portrayals reinforced gender stereotypes and questioned her motives and abilities as a female athlete.

- **Social disapproval:** Switzer's defiance of gender norms and her decision to challenge the norm made her face criticism and condemnation from individuals who viewed her actions as inappropriate or disruptive to the established order. However, she remained resolute in her determination to challenge gender stereotypes.

The journey of Kathrine Switzer, the first woman to officially run the Boston Marathon, is a profound reminder of the resilience and determination that has characterized the history of running. Kathrine Switzer's real-life story is so profound and fascinating. Yet, there is more to running history; exploring it will offer you deeper insight.

The History of Running

The history of running is as old as humanity. When we trace back to when running first started, there isn't a specific date or a named person who was the first runner. Running has played a significant role in human history, culture, and evolution, recounting from ancient hunting practices to modern-day competitive sports. However, there are lots of fascinating milestones that have developed into the sport it is today.

Stone Age Era

Running was a vital skill imbibed by early humans for survival. This is especially true with hunting, where hunters chase prey over long distances. It's also a skill used as the then-common practice of traveling long distances on foot. Covering long distances on foot was a significant advantage that enabled early humans to thrive in diverse environments. In the stone age, there was always a need to run. It wasn't always a choice or something to do for fun. It was a survival instinct.

Several ancient cultures also incorporated running into their ritual processes and ceremonies. It was often used as a form of worship or to commemorate events. For instance, the ancient Greeks held the Olympic Games, where running races were among the main events. Around 700 B.C.E., foot races became a prominent feature of Greek festivals, with athletes competing in various distances as part of religious rituals and celebrations. The most notable was the Olympic Games, which began in 776 B.C.E. The *stadion* race was one of the earliest recorded running events. These games, held every four years, featured a range of athletic contests, including sprinting, long-distance running, and relay races, attracting competitors from across the Greek world and beyond.

Running was also popular in ancient Roman culture. The Romans organized various foot races, including the *stade*, similar to the Greek *stadion* race. Mesopotamian and Egyptian civilizations ran as part of military training and sports competitions. Running was also depicted in artworks and pictograms.

Pre-Modern Era

After the fall of the Roman Empire, organized sports, including running, declined in popularity during the medieval period. Although, running remained a necessary skill for messengers, soldiers, and travelers. During the Renaissance, sports, including running, were revived as people became interested in art. As in the 17th and early to mid-18th centuries, foot races gained popularity in England, with events often held between villages or towns. By the beginning of the modern era, track and field had begun to take shape, laying the foundation for some breakthroughs in running.

Modern Era

The 19th century brought about the officialization of modern athletics. Several organizations were founded within England and the United States. These organizations helped promote running competitions. The modern Olympic Games, inspired by the ancient Greek tradition, were revived in 1896 in Athens, Greece. Running events, including the marathon, became central to the Olympics and other international sports competitions.

Throughout the 20th century, training methods adopted for running have evolved significantly. Scientific research into physiology, nutrition, and biomechanics has led to more effective training programs, helping athletes reach possible peaks in their performances.

Running gained popularity as a recreational activity and exercise in the latter half of the 20th century. Events like marathons, half-marathons, and 5-K races became widespread, attracting participants of all ages and fitness levels.

By 1912, the International Amateur Athletics Federation (IAAF) was founded. The foundation was a move that helped with the convergence of national athletics bodies worldwide. It was governed by its rules and regulations, which still exist today. Later on, on New Year's Day of 1921, the first National Collegiate Athletic Association (NCAA) National Championships were held for men. This was a new level of achievement in the sports world. The first women's athletics added running in the summer games of the same year.

By the 21st century, further technological advancements positively changed the athletic atmosphere, benefiting elite athletes and recreational runners. There were wearable fitness trackers, running apps, and sophisticated running shoes that enhanced training, performance tracking, and injury prevention.

Running events have become platforms for raising awareness and funds for various social and environmental causes. Charity runs, eco-friendly, and virtual races have become popular ways to combine running with activism and community engagement. Running is now considered a global phenomenon, with significant events in cities worldwide. The accessibility of running, combined with the sense of accomplishment and camaraderie it fosters, continues to attract millions of participants globally.

Benefits of Running

Running is beyond the mere movement of the body. But what are the benefits of running for the average runner? Before you start running, it's essential to understand the benefits that await you on this journey. These benefits are transformative experiences that impact every aspect of your well-being.

Physical Benefits

- **Improved cardiovascular health:** Like many other endurance exercises, running strengthens the heart and improves circulation, lowering the risk of heart disease.

- **Weight management:** Running burns calories effectively, aiding in weight loss or maintenance. According to Wheeler (2024), if the right conditions are met, running can burn up to 671 calories in 30 minutes.

- **Stronger muscles and bones:** Regular running helps build and maintain muscle mass and bone density. Its weight-bearing nature strengthens the musculoskeletal system, especially the leg muscles.

- **Enhanced respiratory function:** Running increases lung capacity and efficiency. As you run, your breathing rate and depth increase, training your lungs to work more efficiently. Over time, this improves your respiratory function, making breathing easier during physical activity and rest.

- **Boosted immune system:** Intense exercises like running help flush bacteria out of the lungs and airways, reducing the risk of respiratory infections. Furthermore, exercise promotes the circulation of immune cells and antibodies throughout the body, enhancing the body's ability to detect and respond to pathogens. That is evident as runners often experience fewer sick days and a reduced incidence of common illnesses.

- **Anti-aging benefits:** Studies have shown that consistent running can lower blood pressure and resting heart rate, improve blood sugar control, lower triglycerides, and lower cholesterol. It can also reduce waist circumference and body fat percentage. Improving these health markers can reduce disease risk and help you feel healthier overall (Sayer & Turbett, 2023).

Mental Benefits

- **Stress relief:** Running is a powerful stress reliever, thanks to the release of endorphins, often called "feel-good" hormones, during exercise. Endorphins help reduce stress and anxiety, promote relaxation, and improve mood. The rhythmic motion of running can also have a meditative effect, allowing you to clear your mind and focus on the present moment, further reducing stress levels.

- **Improved sleep:** Regular exercise, including running, has been shown to enhance sleep quality and duration. Running helps to regulate your body's internal clock, known as the circadian rhythm, leading to better sleep-wake cycles. Additionally, the physical exertion of running tires out your body, making it easier to fall asleep and stay asleep throughout the night. Better sleep quality improves mood, cognitive function, and overall well-being.

- **Enhanced cognitive function:** Running has numerous benefits, including improved memory, concentration, and mental clarity. The increased blood flow and oxygen delivery to the brain during exercise stimulate the growth of new neurons and synapses, enhancing cognitive function. Regular running has also been linked to a reduced risk of cognitive decline and neurodegenerative diseases such as Alzheimer's disease in later life.

- **Mood enhancement:** Running profoundly impacts mood regulation and emotional well-being. The release of endorphins during exercise creates a sense of euphoria and happiness, often called the "runner's high." This natural mood boost can help alleviate symptoms of depression, anxiety, and stress, leading to a more positive outlook on life. Additionally, the sense of accomplishment and empowerment that comes from achieving running goals can further enhance mood and self-esteem.

- **Stress management:** Running provides a healthy outlet for stress management, allowing you to channel negative emotions into physical activity. The rhythmic motion of running can be soothing, helping you to process and release pent-up stress and tension. Regular running sessions can build resilience to stress over time, making coping with life's challenges and maintaining emotional balance easier.

Emotional Benefits

- **Increased self-esteem:** Setting and achieving running goals, whether completing a certain distance, improving your pace, or participating in a race, can boost self-esteem and self-confidence. Each milestone you reach reinforces your sense of capability and achievement, empowering you to overcome obstacles on and off the track.

- **Sense of achievement:** Crossing the finish line of a race or accomplishing a personal running milestone instills a profound sense of accomplishment and pride. The dedication and perseverance required to reach your goals cultivate a strong sense of self-worth and fulfillment. Celebrating these achievements with friends, family, or fellow runners further reinforces your sense of belonging and accomplishment within the running community.

- **Connection with nature:** Many runners enjoy connecting with nature while running outdoors. Whether exploring scenic trails, running along the beach, or navigating urban parks, spending time in nature can promote peace, tranquility, and awe. The natural world's sights, sounds, and smells provide a welcome respite from the hustle and bustle of daily life, allowing you to recharge and rejuvenate both physically and emotionally.

- **Social connection:** Running offers numerous opportunities for social connection and camaraderie. Joining a running group, participating in organized races, or running with friends or family can foster meaningful relationships and a sense of belonging. Sharing the running experience with others creates bonds built on mutual support, encouragement, and shared goals, enriching your overall running experience and emotional well-being.

The physical, mental, and emotional benefits of running are interconnected, creating a holistic approach to well-being that extends beyond the miles you log.

Whether you aim to improve your physical fitness, boost your mood, or cultivate a greater sense of purpose and connection, running offers a powerful pathway to achieving your goals and living a healthier, happier life.

My Personal Connection

Running has changed my life in numerous positive ways. It has sparked a passion and drive I never imagined resided within me. Through my wins and losses as a runner, I've built an unwavering confidence and tenacity that has helped me to face life's challenges head-on. Running has been my steadfast companion in navigating the complexities of mental health, providing a therapeutic outlet that has helped me confront and conquer depression and anxiety. Each stride has been a step towards healing, offering clarity of mind and a sense of purpose that transcends the physical benefits of this empowering practice.

While my running journey has been decorated with occasional setbacks, including injuries and unpleasant "did not finish" (DNF) moments, these challenges have only fortified my resolve. They have taught me invaluable lessons about resilience, perseverance, and the importance of self-care and recovery. Running has instilled in me the desire to push through adversity, embrace the process, and continue moving forward with unwavering determination.

So, this guide is quite personal to me. I invite you to embrace the transformative power of running and discover the profound personal connection that awaits you on this empowering journey. It will enrich your life and nourish your soul. Here are a few things to note as you navigate your way toward building an unstoppable spirit when it comes to running:

- **Don't stop when things get tough:** Imagine starting a 3000-meter race and stopping somewhere around 2,500 meters. That is what giving up your running dream feels like, especially if you've been doing the work and have not yet gotten results. In life, challenges are inevitable, so pushing through tough moments builds resilience and strengthens resolve. The actual test of strength lies in persevering when the going gets tough.

- **Achieving your goals takes hard work:** Setting ambitious goals in the running requires dedication and intentional efforts. A combination of consistent training, discipline, and a willingness to push beyond your comfort zone are all catalysts for turning your running aspirations into achievements and medals.

- **Comparison is the thief of joy:** Running is a personal journey, so you should endeavor to measure your progress against your capabilities, not against that of others. This will ensure a fulfilling and enjoyable experience.

- **You're stronger than you think:** Running often reveals an untapped well of strength and endurance within yourself. Daring to push beyond your perceived limits demonstrates that the mind and body are capable of more than you may have initially believed.

- **Everything is mental:** Running is as connected to the mind as it is to the body. Mastering the inner dialogue, overcoming doubts, and maintaining focus are crucial for success on the track of sprints and life.

- **You do "have the time":** Prioritizing running amidst busy schedules highlights the importance of making time for what truly matters. With determination and efficient time management, there's always time to pursue passions and goals. So, if you've been procrastinating, this is the right time to wear those running shoes.

- **Working as a team will lead to success.** When you run alongside your training partners or receive support from your coaches and mentors, teamwork fosters growth and pushes you further towards your goals than doing it alone.

- **If you wait for the "perfect time," you'll never accomplish anything:** Waiting for the perfect conditions or timing often leads to missed opportunities. Embracing imperfection and taking action is critical to progress and success, even in uncertainty.

- **You define you:** Running empowers you to determine your journey and success metrics. Embracing your strengths, weaknesses, and aspirations allows authentic self-expression and fulfillment.

- **Just because you lose doesn't mean you're a loser:** As far as life is concerned, setbacks and defeats are inevitable. Failure does not define your worth, but your response to setbacks does.

- **There are no shortcuts, hacks, or tricks:** Running teaches the core value of hard work and dedication. Depending on how you want to see it, the news is that there are no quick fixes or shortcuts to achieving meaningful results. You earn success through consistent effort and a willingness to embark on the journey, regardless of how challenging it may be.

What have you learned, rounding off this chapter? I believe you've been left breathless by the sheer grit and determination displayed by Kathrine Switzer, who refused to be confined to the sidelines.

However, Kathrine Switzer is just one of the pioneers who triumphed against severe opposition. In the next chapter, we will look at more "*Pioneers of the Path*," such as Joan Benoit Samuelson and Grete Waitz. You will explore the untold stories of these fearless trailblazers whose footsteps have continued to echo through time, inspiring a global movement of female empowerment in the running.

Chapter 2:

Pioneers of the Path

Triumph over adversity that's what the marathon is all about. Nothing in life can't triumph after that. —Kathrine Switzer

Dozens, hundreds, and thousands of women have embarked on milestone moments and actions in running, making them astounding pioneers for other women looking to embrace running as part of their everyday lives! These pioneers have created a remarkable path possible through their determination, devotion, resilience, and mind-blowing achievements, defying how society perceived women.

From the undefeated Joan Benoit Samuelson to the remarkable achievements of Grete Waitz, these women didn't just make history; they created and smoothened the way for future generations of women. What challenges did they face, how did they weather the storm, and how remarkable was their impact? You will find answers to all these questions in this chapter! Delving into their lives, you'll discover the outstanding spirit of human nature and the zeal for a more equitable and just world.

Barriers to Women's Running

Before the 1970s, women were regarded as weaker vessels who should steer clear of sports, not to mention running long-distance races. In fact, in 1896, when the modern Olympics came into existence, women were not allowed to participate.

Then came 1900, for the first time, women were privileged to participate in Olympic sports like golfing, croquet, and sailing, but they were still deterred from running. 1928 came, and luckily, women could run races like 100 meters and 800 meters, but some collapsed before even reaching the final line, convincing critics that they were no match for running.

After the decision of the International Olympic Committee (IOC) was made in 1938, women were only allowed to run 100-meter races. Then, they started allowing them to participate in other races. This was a significant step forward, but it was just the beginning. In 1948, the 200-meter race was included, and in 1964, the 400-meter race was added. 1960, the 800-meter race was added, but the 1500-meter race was delayed till 1972. These changes did not just come by chance. They resulted from years of advocacy and activism by women determined to have their voices heard and their abilities recognized.

Just around that time, so many women were going over the board in the marathon mold in the US. For example, Violet Piercy was the first woman to run the marathon race in 1926. We also have Kathrine Switzer, who was famous then and participated in the Boston Marathon in 1967. Next, 1972 came, and women were permitted to participate in the Boston and New York marathons.

Since then, we've had several amazing women who have shown that women should not be belittled. One of the fantastic women was Grete Waitz in 1979, the first woman to run a sub 2:30 marathon. Not only did she participate, but she won her second New York City Marathon with a time of 2:27:33. However, as time went by, other women joined and performed excellently, able to beat the records set by Grete Waitz. These goal-oriented women are Joan Benoit, Ingrid Kristiansen, Tegla Loroupe, Naoko Takahashi, and others who have been setting the record until now. Recently, the record was reset by another woman, Brigit Kosgei, with a 2:14:04. Her achievement is a testament to the continued progress and determination of women in marathon running. It's truly remarkable to witness the evolution of women's marathon races over the past four decades. It's a testament to the pioneers who refused to give up despite the odds and challenges. It's safe to say that without them, the landscape of your career and the lives of many others would be vastly different.

What amazes me the most about this new wave of women's acceptance in sports is how women have not only been participating in ultramarathon races but also winning them.

Consider a study made by the University of Cape Town in 1997 that proved a hypothesis that women who participated in ultra-marathon races are more resistant to tiredness than men who are equally trained for marathon races. The report confirmed that about the 90k distance, women begin to beat men during the race (Burdick, 2013).

Joan Benoit Samuelson's Olympic Victory

Joan Benoit Samuelson is a champion in marathon running. She made history when she made a dangerous early break at the inaugural women's 1984 Olympic Marathon in Los Angeles. She ran without competitors for the last 21 miles of the race, and she became prominent after receiving the gold medal. Benoit can be seen as one of the legends of marathon races due to her several wins, love for running, and devotion. Joan Benoit Samuelson's story emphasizes the need never to give up!

Benoit started running just after she recovered from an injury she sustained while skiing. While at Bowdoin College, she participated in track and cross-country, and while she was in her senior year, she participated in the 1979 Boston Marathon.

With a time of 2:35:15, Benoit emerged as the winner, breaking a record. Benoit also beat the world record in 1983 in Boston when she ran a 2:22:43.

Joan Benoit was passionate and dedicated to running. Imagine participating in bodily-demanding work just after a major surgery. That is exactly what Benoit did. She participated in the Olympic Trials race and won 17 days after her arthroscopic knee surgery. What a woman she is!

Benoit went on to participate in the first Olympic marathon for women in August 1984. Remember, the IOC had stopped women from participating in the event because they had an opinion that marathon races were detrimental to women's health. It was a beautiful morning then, and the sport was held at the Santa Monica City College track. Then, the temperature was quite chilling, so even when the race began, Benoit, with the other participants, continued in a tight group for the first three miles. Benoit feared being in tight or narrow spaces, so she broke away from the group during the fourth mile.

As the race continued, she gave the other participants a wide gap. Some people believed she couldn't keep up with the same energy for the rest of the race, but Benoit never gave the other contestants a chance to outrun her. She determined she was going to win and put her mind to it. After 26 miles, she came out of the tunnel into the stadium to finish the last lap, and she was greeted with the sound of 77,000 people clapping and cheering her up. Even though she was weak, she didn't allow all the cheers from the crowd to get in her head; she continued running. When it was time for the last 299 meters, she waved her cap to the cheering crowd and then crossed the finish line. Benoit successfully won the gold medal with a time of 2:24:52, beating her closest competitor just by a minute. What made her win quite fascinating was because of the injuries and hurdles she overcame in her bid to come out as the winner.

Impact of Joan Benoit Samuelson's Win on Women's Sports History

Benoit's win not only brought her career to the limelight but also impacted women's sports in a significant way. When she emerged as the winner in 1984, many started readjusting their view of female athletes. Without these beautiful women in sports history, women would just be able to watch sports and probably not be privileged to participate.

For several years, some people thought women could not participate in races beyond 1,500 meters. "They're probably just going to faint" were common demeaning expressions. Unfortunately, this assumption was a reality 40 years ago until women like Joan Benoit and several others changed the narratives of women's sports.

Fast-forward to the early 1980s. Even though women were allowed to run marathon distances, they were not allowed to run more than three and three-quarter laps at the Olympic Games. The reason was that they perceived women as being too feeble for long races.

As time passed, a woman who was a two-time marathon world record holder set up a committee for women going for gold at long-distance races. Nike supported her, and she was assisted by her close friend and colleague, Joan Benoit.

The two females were supported by Nike, who fully funded them, and connections from well-placed runners. The efforts of Benoit and her team members were successful because the 3000-meter and marathon were included for women in Los Angeles around the year 1984. Fifty participants toed the start of the game on the 5 of August. After about 2:15:32 into the game, Joan Benoit made sure that nobody ever questioned the ability of women to take part in marathon races.

Benoit's performance wasn't just breathtaking because she was a woman, but because her performance in the race surpassed 13 of the 20 men who were winners. Around that time in Southern California, the heat was relatively high, but that didn't stop Benoit. She finished the race a minute and a half faster, regardless of the arthroscopic knee surgery she had three months before the game.

The effect of Benoit's race was felt even longer than summer. It paved the way for female athletes worldwide to fully participate in track races of their choice without any restriction. Even though the fight for female inclusion existed before her arrival, with her, everything started to take a beautiful turn.

Grete Waitz's Marathon Dominance and Legacy

Great people made the impossible possible! Grete Waitz is one of those women who did the unimaginable. She was able to personify this attribute throughout her life. She was exceptional in everything she did, and most of her accomplishments were often kept from the public. She maintained excellence for quite a long time and made excellence seem like something very easy to pull off.

Waitz never wavered in supporting sporting activities, children's programs, and cancer research. Several people were oblivious to her good works, as they were only aware of her deeds that were revealed to the public. She wasn't someone who loved the praise of people or someone who did good because of public attention. She deserved every good thing, even in abundance.

How Grete Waitz Impacted Women's Sports History

Waitz was the first woman in the world-class track to begin a marathon. She decided to run her first marathon in 1978 in New York. She didn't just emerge as the winner but set a world record. Isn't that fascinating? After that race, she decided she wouldn't participate in any marathon race again, but as time passed, she changed her mind. She went back to New York in 1979 and beat the record she set by reducing it by 5 minutes. It's in history that Waitz was the first female marathoner to break her 2:30 with her new record of 2:27:33. Our superwoman, Waitz, beat her record once again in 1980, and she became 9 minutes and 6 seconds faster than other female athletes in history.

The only major event Waitz didn't participate in was the Olympic Championship. Still, she participated in other significant events, like Joan Benoit's gold in Los Angeles, which took place in 1984, and she won a silver medal. About 10 weeks after the marathon in Los Angeles, she emerged as the winner of the 1984 New York City Marathon. She also won this marathon in 1985, 1986, and 1988.

How Grete Waitz Went From Being a Winner to a Chairwoman

In 1988, Waitz emerged as the winner in her 9th marathon race, and after participating in her 10th race, she came out 4th. After that, she retired from strenuous competitions, even though she participated in the New York City Marathon with Fred Lebow, the then president of New York Road Runners (NYRR), and both completed the race together in 5:32:34. Following her retirement, Waitz accumulated numerous accolades. Transitioning into a coaching role, she mentored noteworthy athletes such as Liz McColgan, the victor of the 1991 New York City Marathon, among others. Additionally, she undertook the role of organizing the annual Grete's Run in Norway, a well-attended event uniting thousands of women. A strong advocate for workplace well-being, she actively supported initiatives promoting health and fitness while also spearheading fundraising efforts for charitable organizations like CARE International and the Special Olympics.

Waitz was later honored to become the chairwoman of the NYRR foundation in 1998, which has become the prestigious Rising New York Road Runners. This youth fitness scheme now supports about 250,000 children in New York City and abroad. As usual, she decided not to just be a figurehead but to become an active member and ensured she regularly associated with the children. She went to the parties organized, ran with the children, and supported them at their races when she was in New York. When she wasn't there, she wrote letters for the children's newsletter, personally replied to the letters of the kids who wrote to her, and assisted them in program development.

Grete Waitz's Battles With Cancer

Unfortunately for Waitz, she was diagnosed with cancer in 2005. She dealt with this battle the same way she gently dealt with an Olympic final or a world record event. She diverted her attention to fighting against the brutal battle; luckily, she had the support of many others to help her during those trying times. Waitz became the founder of Aktiv Krect in 2007, then set up a partnership between the foundation and Adidas, which had been her supporter from day one. They channeled 5% of their earnings from her clothing brand, which was about $1.25 million yearly. The money was used to provide cancer-specialist hospitals with equipment like PET imagining scanners that could help treat cancer effectively.

Waitz was beautiful in every way; she never allowed her condition to weigh her down and always spoke to other cancer patients and educated them on the need to exercise.

Personal Connection

The community and society you live in play a significant role in making you achieve your goals. When I first started ultras, folks around me thought I was crazy. They never stopped reminding me of the hazard I was putting myself into, and they made it a duty to discourage me. With the constant pressure, I was close to giving up on my dream and being a people pleaser. Fortunately, I came across another community and resources that were a massive support system.

They never stopped encouraging me to think big and go out of my way to achieve my dream. Reflecting on this turning point, I can't imagine how my life would have turned out if I had listened to people who tried to destroy my dreams. One thing I'm sure of is that I wouldn't be where I am today. I could have never dreamed of running 50 miles in one day if I hadn't joined the community that I did. Most importantly, I would have never met the amazing people I have in my life right now. It's wild how other people can influence our growth and progression.

I remain forever grateful to those who brought out the best in me and made me see my possibilities. I'm thankful to those who never wanted my dream to see the light of day because they were a source of motivation and perseverance. I needed to show the world I could be whoever I wanted. Even though I'm not Joan Benoit Samuelson or Grete Waitz, who were terrific women who paved the way for me and others, it brings me so much joy to see others decide to take up the mantle after seeing what they've accomplished. That's the beauty in all of this—the ability to show others the depths they can reach if only they broke out from their fears because fear only brings bondage.

The pioneers you have examined should remind you of the importance of resilience and setting achievable goals. Let this motivate you to be tenacious and courageous with whatever you put your mind to. You are achieving your lifelong dream, my darling!

In the next chapter, we will explore the stories of women who not only followed the path created by these pioneers but also set new standards, changing the narrative of women's running.

Chapter 3:

Breaking Records

I don't run away from a challenge because I am afraid. Instead, I run towards it because the only way to escape fear is to trample it beneath your feet. —Nadia Comaneci

To break world records in running, not only do women need a fast course but also top talent, and excitedly, we've had inspiring women who shattered glass ceilings and set world records, giving hope to many women around the globe.

From the early pioneers who fought against societal norms and expectations to our present-day champions who are setting new records every day, women in sports have continually set new boundaries of virtue and greatness.

You can learn a great deal of lessons from these women, and that's the focus of this chapter! You will learn about women who defied all odds to become winners and how they've been able to impact future generations positively. Every single broken record attests to the fact that you can achieve anything with relentless devotion and out-of-this-world talents.

As you examine the remarkable wins of these women, you'll unmask tales of exceptional braveness, desire, and the uncompromising chase of success.

Challenging Societal Norms and Expectations

Today, both men and women participate in sporting competitions. If you've ever had the opportunity to play any sports, there's a probability that you've had one very influential female athlete who inspires you to reach your peak. However, that was not the case some years back. While there is still some discrimination against women's involvement in sports, it can never be compared to the hardship they faced in the past, and we cannot write that off. Looking back at how things were and how they have evolved to what they are now will deepen your appreciation for the women who put in all the effort. The issue of inequality in ancient sports is one. Of course, it's not news that women were not always allowed to play sports, but when exactly did this turning point occur?

First, Homer's *Odyssey* suggests that women should come together to play ball. Some ancient Greek festivals allowed women to participate in foot races and horseback riding at the Olympics. For the Spartans, it was customary for women to participate in sports like discus, javelin-throwing, and wrestling.

Other cultures, such as the Native Americans and some other indigenous traditions, have also allowed women to exhibit their athletic tendencies. In addition, the Server people were involved in *Laamb*, a traditional kind of wrestling that allowed women to participate until it was stopped in the 20th century.

Let's dive into Victorian Western Europe, a time when society perceived women as being feeble and helpless. There were several myths that a woman's body was too weak to be subject to any form of stress. They had this idea that sports could drain up a woman's energy and render her barren or bear wimpy children. However, some women started playing tennis and golf at some clubs, and society began accepting women's participation in sports.

After some time, women started showing their capabilities in the world of sports. Some found it hard to believe how these women were shaking things up due to the tales that had been imprinted in their heads about females wanting to intrude into the world of males. So, for a considerable amount of time in the 20th century, people hated the shapes that athletic women had.

They thought they looked extra masculine, and they never understood why women would appreciate having muscles or destroying their feminine nature. In short, before we were able to watch women participate freely in sports, it was so challenging for females in the past because not only were they prevented from participating, but societal norms were also against them participating in professional running.

The Female Body in Running

Mothers often add lots of milk to their children's diet to help their children grow strong bones. However, this isn't the case with adults. The amount of milk you drink as an adult doesn't determine how strong your bones will be. About 10 million people in the United States have osteoporosis, a condition that makes the bone weak, and this isn't an exception for athletes (Leigey et al., 2009). We all know that running is a form of exercise, and exercises strengthen the bones; however, it's a sport that causes a high number of stress fractures. So, every runner, especially women, should work hard to protect their bones to ensure they are strong and healthy because a woman's body is built differently from a man's, and you have a responsibility to keep yourself healthy.

Osteoporosis is like a silent killer. You often won't even know anything is wrong with your bones; they might still be as strong as usual until the condition eats deep. Most people with osteoporosis have complained of bone breaks, usually in the wrist, spine, or hips, and these bone breaks can happen from something so little, like sneezing. Therefore, women above 50 must go for a bone mineral density test.

The purpose of the test is to know the density of the bone, and female runners need to have a strong bone density and strength because stress fractures range from 0.7% to 15.6% of sports injuries. A stress fracture is caused by several reasons, like low bone muscle density, overworking oneself, or even wearing tight-fitting sneakers. So, if you're taking up a sport like running, your health is paramount.

Paula Radcliffe's World Record and Influence

Paula Radcliffe, on 13 April 2020, became a source of inspiration to many. She emerged as the winner of the London marathon with a time of 2:15:25. What's more jaw-dropping is that she beat her world record of 2:17:18, which she set in Chicago. If you're a guru in marathon races, you'd know that currently, in the world of sports, that distance isn't anything small; it's enormous.

Radcliffe's race in the London Marathon in 2003 still shocks most sports enthusiasts. During that time, the director of the race and a one-time 10,000-meter world champion called her performance the most fantastic marathon race he had ever witnessed in his lifetime. Radcliffe was also able to maintain that title for quite a long time. For about 12 years after her outstanding performance, no other female has been able to break her record of finishing a marathon within 3 minutes. Nobody! Even now, Radcliffe is among the 3 fastest women's marathons in sports history.

Some people never stopped wondering how a woman from Cheshire, with a somewhat awkward manner of walking, beat the world record in a spot that was mostly filled with East Africans. One aspect that people keep hammering about her race in London is that two men were also in the marathon race. How was it even possible that she overtook two men?

Taking a look at how Radcliffe prepared for the race is quite interesting. The way she was able to withstand pain is quite remarkable. Gerard Hartmann, who was her physiotherapist for a long time, lived with her for a couple of weeks and had an interview with the Guardian in 2013. She said (Kessel, 2013):

> I've worked with 63 Olympic medalists and nobody from Haile Gebrselassie to Kelly Holmes, who on the treatment table could ever take that level of pain. She would hurt me rather than allow me to hurt her. She would break me down because I'd have to go so deep into the sinews, I would have to ice my thumbs afterward because I was in such pain. (para. 11)

Radcliffe couldn't just withstand pain, but she also cared about her health. You'd often see her working out not to become more fit but to heal her wounds quickly. One enlightening statistic about Radcliffe is that she increased her running economy by more than 15% throughout her career. Running economy is how much energy is required to power an athlete, and it's imperative in one's career as a runner. She may have appeared awkwardly, but she trained herself to use her fuel wisely. Radcliffe considered her head more important than other parts of her body. Why? An athlete has to be innovative, and it all comes from the head. She was once asked what time she was going to run the first half during the London marathon, and she replied that she didn't have an idea. However, her goal in the marathon was to run a negative split, which meant running faster in the race's second half. She never limited herself to one tactic throughout her career, claiming, "I run how I feel like" (Caesar, 2015, para. 11).

Paula Radcliffe's Influence on Long-distance Running and Her Role in Inspiring Both Women and Men in the Sport

When we talk about indigenous female athletes, Paula Radcliffe's name will forever be mentioned. For the past 20 years on the track, in all of her races, Radcliffe has always been a dominant athlete, and nobody has been able to beat her world record of 2:15:25, which was set during the London Marathon in April 2003. Let's take a look into the life of Radcliffe and how she has been able to influence long-distance running in her way.

She became a member of her first athletics club at age 11, Bedford and County Athletics Club, and when she was 16, she took part in the World Cross-Country Championships. She also received several awards as an athlete, such as an MBE award in 2002 and an award from the BBC's Sports Personality of the Year in 2002. Apart from her holding the world record time, Radcliffe is among the three women who ran the quickest times in sports history, and since then, no woman has been able to beat her world record.

Radcliffe has also been a source of inspiration to several women across the world. The truth is, who wouldn't draw inspiration from such a noble woman? While she was 14,

Radcliffe got asthma, and that didn't in any way stop her from becoming one of the best. One lesson from Radcliffe's condition is that you shouldn't let your current predicament stop you from achieving your goals. Asthma didn't stop her from working out regularly, so nothing should be able to stop you. Once she set the world record in London, many people became interested in buying trainers and clothing for several months. Radcliffe significantly impacted the British people, and the trainers and equipment she used were sold out quickly. She quickly became the role model for others interested in distance running, and at that time, several people suddenly became interested in jogging.

Radcliffe's legacy has inspired many and is still inspiring others. Whether you're running as a hobby or you're interested in joining the athletics club, we all can enjoy the benefits of running.

Florence Griffith Joyner's Sprinting Success and Cultural Impact

Let's look into the world of another talented female athlete, Florence Griffith, who started running when she was just 7 years old. However, she had to stop running at age 19 to help her family. Fortunately for her, Bob Kersee, a Sprint coach, found her while working as a bank teller and helped her get into UCLA. During the 1984 Olympic Games in her hometown, Los Angeles, she won a silver medal in the 200-meter. However, what attracted people and the press were her long and specially painted fingernails. She then married a 1974 triple jump Olympic champion, Al Joyner, and then changed her name to that of her husband's, Florence Griffith Joyner, hence her nickname "Flo-Jo."

Griffith Joyner made a world record on 16 of July 1988 in the US when she ran a 100-meter race within 10.49 seconds, beating the former record of 10.79 seconds. What's more fascinating is that her record was better than that of the men in several countries like Ireland, New Zealand, and Turkey.

Griffith Joyner's groundbreaking achievements didn't just stop there; she broke the Olympic record at the Seoul Olympic Games and emerged as the winner in a wind-aided 10.54. Just 4 days later, she beat the world record for 200-meter, and unbelievably, after 100 minutes, she set another record with 21.34 seconds. Till now, her 100-meter and 200-meter records have not been broken by anyone. At the Olympic games in Seoul, she participated in both relay races and won her third gold medal in the 4x100-meter and 4x400-meter races.

Florence Griffith Joyner's Lasting Legacy in the World of Athletics and Beyond

For about 30 years, Florence Griffith Joyner held the world record she set at the 1988 Olympic Games, and on July 16, she won the 100-meter race and was given the title of the fastest woman in the world. After that, she won three gold medals as a U.S. team member and set a new record for the 200-meter race. Till today, no one has been able to beat her records. No one has come close.

Apart from her numerous achievements in women's sports, Flo-Jo has a legacy of being one of the most fashionable women ever in sports history. She was well known for her beautiful, bright tracksuits and long nails, which she wore proudly. She was very proud of her style, and till now, nobody has been able to match her sense of style and fashion.

Flo-Jo also appeared in many magazines like Jet, Time, and Sports Illustrated. Apart from her achievements as an athlete, what attracted many was her confidence and unmatchable poise. She wasn't just a track star but also a designer and a beautician. Flo-Jo was dauntless and in every way fashionable; no one came close.

Griffith Joyner's impact remains till now. Recently, the phenomenal Serena Williams made use of Griffith Joyner's fierceness. Williams is another female that's doing just well in her career. At the Australian Open in 2021, she made a double victory over her opponent in the first round. After her achievements, she acknowledged Flo-Jo by wearing a multi-colored Nike tracksuit with only one leg.

Personal Connection

Sometimes, we can be our own worst enemy! There are times when we allow doubt and insecurities to set in; if only we knew the possibilities we could achieve when all forms of negativity are gone. I have struggled with this throughout my running career, always setting a limit that "I could never achieve." The funny thing is that the limit started at a half-marathon (13.1 miles). I ran a half-marathon and immediately told everyone I had fun but could never run a full marathon (26.2 miles). Then, a year or so later, I found myself training and crossing the finish line of my first marathon. I was hooked but never dreamed of anything further.

I found out about ultramarathons about eight years ago, and again, I found myself saying I could never run farther than a marathon. Thankfully, I have running friends who saw things differently and convinced me to try. I nervously agreed but still stated that one 50-K and I'm done, just enough to call myself an ultrarunner and say I did it. I look back and laugh now because even though I still struggle with those doubts and self-limitations, I do have 7 50-Ks and 5 50-milers under my belt, and I will continue to train for even longer distances in the future. It's okay to be afraid, but what you should never do is allow your fears to overwhelm you. You're worth more than you could ever imagine, so do not allow anything to hold you back from trying.

Looking deeply into the career and lifestyle of incredible female athletes like Paula Radcliffe and Florence Griffith Joyner, one lesson we can learn is perseverance and sheer dedication. Never allow your current predicament to stop you from achieving your lifelong dream. Let this be your cue to set new standards and defy all odds to reach your goal.

Just like there's no present without a past, these women have paved the way for a continuous evolution of women's running. In the next chapter, we'll look at the stories of contemporary runners who are carrying on the mantle and keeping the flames alive. These women have also set new ground and have been a source of inspiration to women across the world in the 21st century.

Chapter 4:

A New Era

One step at a time. One round at a time. Know your why. It's just one step at a time. Whether that's a race or in real life. You just have to know your why. —Allyson Felix

The Evolution of Competitive Women's Running

The competitive women's running world has seen incredible changes over the last few decades. In the past, women were often not allowed to participate in many major races. Today, female athletes are breaking records and inspiring people everywhere, including myself. This feat has been particularly possible due to the evolutionary changes witnessed by this sport, leading to massive advancements from the late 20th century.

Technological Advancements

One of the most significant advancements in women's running has been in footwear. The late 20th century saw the introduction of more specialized running shoes designed to improve performance and reduce injury risk. England's first known running shoe from the mid-1860s was a leather dress shoe with nails for spikes. Real improvements began in the early 20th century when Keds and Converse started making athletic shoes with rubber soles. In the late 1930s, German brothers Rudolph and Adi Dassler made running shoes together before splitting up to create Puma and Adidas. Since then, new materials like foam, polyester, and carbon fiber have continued to improve running shoe technology.

Before the advent of high-tech recording machines, a photograph of the finish line was usually captured to determine the winner. For example, a very complicated 1948 Olympic race had to observe a photo finish to determine the winner closely. This was because determining the winner from the top two racers with mere human eyes was impossible.

Wearable technology has revolutionized how athletes train and compete. Devices like GPS watches, heart rate monitors, and fitness trackers allow runners to monitor their pace, distance, heart rate, and other vital statistics in real time. Brands like Garmin, Polar, and Apple have developed sophisticated devices that offer advanced analytics, helping runners optimize their training programs and race strategies.

Training Methodologies

Training methodologies have also evolved with the advent of new technologies and research. High-altitude training simulators, advanced treadmills, and virtual training platforms have provided athletes with several training environments. For instance, treadmills with variable inclines and resistance settings allow runners to simulate different race conditions.

Virtual platforms like Zwift offer interactive and engaging training methods, providing real-time feedback and competitive elements that enhance motivation and performance.

Increasing Visibility of Women's Sports

Think back just a few years, and you'd find women's sports buried under layers of coverage dedicated mostly to men's competitions. But now, it's a different story. According to Forbes, the media attention to women's sports has nearly tripled in just five years (Darvin, 2023). Why? Well, it's partly thanks to us, the viewers, who are hungry for a diverse range of sporting content. Plus, with technology advancing, there are more ways to catch the action, from traditional TV to streaming platforms. Social media has also become a game-changer, giving athletes a direct line to fans and helping boost their profiles. As we see more of them in action, stereotypes are being shattered, and respect for women in sports is growing.

Allyson Felix's Achievements and Advocacy

Allyson Felix's journey in athletics began in Los Angeles, California, where she was born on November 18, 1985. Her interest in track and field sparked in high school, and her natural talent quickly became obvious. With a lean frame and quick legs sprint, Felix dominated high school competitions, earning the nickname "Chicken Legs" due to her slight build. However, her speed was undeniable, and she soon got the whole nation's attention.

Felix's international debut was nothing short of spectacular. At the 2004 Athens Olympics, she won her first Olympic medal—a silver in the 200-meter. This marked the beginning of a stellar career. In the 2008 Beijing Olympics, she secured another silver in the 200-meter. Still, she showcased her versatility and team spirit by winning her first Olympic gold as part of the USA 4x400-meter relay team.

The peak of her performance in the 200-meter came at the 2012 London Olympics, where she won gold. Felix's dominance extended beyond the Olympics; she claimed 3 consecutive World Championships in the 200-meter from 2005 to 2009.

Her prowess was not limited to individual events. Felix was a critical member of the U.S. relay teams, winning 6 Olympic gold medals: 4 in the 4x400-meter relay (2008, 2012, 2016, and 2021) and 2 in the 4x100-meter relay (2012 and 2016). These achievements made her the only female track star to win 7 Olympic gold medals.

Beyond her career as a track star, Felix has been a powerful advocate for maternity rights and gender equality in sports. Her advocacy became particularly prominent after she faced serious challenges during her pregnancy. In 2018, Felix gave birth to her daughter, Camryn, via an emergency C-section at 32 weeks due to severe preeclampsia. This experience profoundly impacted her perspective on athletes' rights, particularly for women.

Felix's influence also extends into broader fitness and youth sports initiatives. She served on President Obama's Council for Fitness, Sports, and Nutrition, playing an important role in setting physical fitness standards for public school districts. Her commitment to promoting active lifestyles among young people is evident in her involvement with organizations like LA84, where she works to ensure that youth have access to quality sports programs.

While her life revolves around athletics and advocacy, Felix enjoys simpler pleasures. She is known for her baking talents, particularly her delicious cinnamon rolls and German chocolate cake, which reflect her love for creating and sharing with others.

Allyson Felix's Advocacy for Pregnant Athletes and Her Stance Against Nike

In 2019, Felix's courage and determination came to the forefront when she publicly challenged Nike, her sponsor, over their treatment of pregnant athletes. Felix revealed that Nike had proposed a 70% pay cut in her contract renewal after she became pregnant, and they refused to guarantee protections for her and other pregnant athletes. Her openness about the situation drew serious media attention and sparked controversies about the rights of female athletes.

She took her stance against Nike to a new level by joining with other athletes like Alysia Montaño and Kara Goucher. Together, they advocated for contractual changes to prevent companies from penalizing female athletes for becoming mothers. This collective stand against one of the biggest names in sportswear led to a significant policy shift at Nike. The company announced that it would no longer apply performance-related reductions for 18 months around pregnancy, setting a new standard in the industry.

Felix's advocacy didn't stop with Nike. She continued to use her platform to push for broader changes in sports and society. Her efforts have led to increased awareness and dialogue about the challenges faced by female athletes, including the need for better support systems and equitable treatment. Her story inspired other athletes to speak up and demand fair treatment. In short, she gave every sportswoman a voice against poor treatment.

By challenging and changing unfair practices, Felix has helped to establish a more supportive and inclusive framework for female athletes. This includes better maternity protections, more equitable sponsorship agreements, and increased visibility and recognition of women's sports. In her latest advocacy campaign, Felix is heading to the 2024 Olympics, not to compete on the track, but to launch the Olympic Village's first nursery. This nursery will be designed as an area with privacy for mother's to breastfeed, as well as a community area where caregivers can engage with their children away from the chaos of the events but less isolated from other athletes and their families.

Allyson Felix's Support for Female Athletes and the Founding of Saysh

Following her public battle with Nike over maternity protections, Felix realized the need for athletic gear that genuinely catered to the unique needs of female athletes. This realization set her on a journey she never anticipated: creating her own athletic footwear company, Saysh.

In June 2021, Felix launched Saysh by introducing the Saysh One sneaker. These shoes aren't just a scaled-down version of men's shoes; they're designed specifically for women's feet, focusing on fit, comfort, and performance. The launch wasn't just about footwear but about empowering women and making a statement. The brand's "I Know My Place" tagline boldly asserts that women belong in every space, including sports and business.

Allyson Felix pointed out that men's and women's feet differ. Women have wider feet, different arch heights, and unique shapes around the balls of their feet. They also have different leg angles, known as Q-angles. Plus, during pregnancy, hormonal changes can make women's feet grow. That's why Saysh offers a special return policy for new moms. Unlike most shoe companies that make smaller versions of men's shoes for women, Saysh designs shoes specifically for women's feet right from the start.

Running Throughout Pregnancy

Pregnancy is a beautiful event, but it can have an effect on your running. During pregnancy, a woman's body undergoes significant changes from head to toe. Pregnant runners take their fair share of the positives and risks involved in running with a baby maturing in their womb.

In case you are wondering if it is safe to run during pregnancy, research has shown that women who run consistently before pregnancy have a greater tolerance for running when pregnant. However, you should remember that every woman is unique. So, it is important to consult a doctor regularly throughout pregnancy to rule out any possible complications that could be worsened by running.

Positive Impacts of Running on Pregnancy

There are many positive impacts running can have that a pregnant runner must be aware of, such as:

- **Easier labor and delivery:** Regular exercise, including running, during pregnancy can help strengthen the muscles needed for labor and delivery. Running helps keep the pelvic floor muscles toned, which may contribute to easier labor and a smoother delivery process. The cardiovascular endurance and muscle strength built through running can also help pregnant women cope better with the physical demands of childbirth.

- **Reduced risk of complications:** Maintaining a consistent running routine throughout pregnancy can help reduce the risk of certain complications, such as gestational diabetes and preeclampsia. Regular exercise promotes better blood circulation, which can help prevent blood pressure issues and improve overall health during pregnancy. Additionally, staying active can aid in managing weight gain and promoting healthy fetal development.

- **Less risk of depression:** Running has been shown to have mood-boosting effects, thanks to the release of endorphins, also known as "feel-good" hormones. For pregnant women, regular physical activity can help alleviate stress, anxiety, and symptoms of depression.

- **Boosted fetal brain development:** Research suggests that maternal exercise, including running, may positively affect fetal brain development. Regular physical activity during pregnancy can increase blood flow to the placenta, providing essential nutrients and oxygen to the developing baby's brain. This could result in improved cognitive function and neurological development in utero.

Risks of Running for Pregnancy

While there are many positives, it is important for women to understand the risks associated with running during pregnancy, such as:

- **Overheating:** The hormonal changes and increased blood volume during pregnancy can make expectant mothers more prone to overheating when running. Elevated body temperature can pose risks to both the mother and the baby, potentially leading to dehydration, heat exhaustion, or even heatstroke. Pregnant runners should take precautions to avoid overheating by staying hydrated, wearing breathable clothing, and exercising during cooler times.

- **Dehydration:** Running while pregnant can increase the risk of dehydration due to greater fluid loss through sweat and increased body demand for water. Dehydration can have adverse effects on maternal health and may even impact fetal development. Pregnant runners should prioritize staying well-hydrated before, during, and after their runs and consider carrying a water bottle filled with chilled water with them.

- **Low blood sugar:** Changes in hormone levels and metabolism during pregnancy can sometimes result in fluctuations in blood sugar levels, leading to hypoglycemia or low blood sugar. Running without adequate fueling can worsen this risk, potentially causing dizziness, weakness, or fainting.

- **Complications from preexisting conditions:** Pregnancy may exacerbate certain preexisting conditions in athletes, such as bone density loss, anemia, pelvic floor dysfunction, incontinence, and musculoskeletal problems. The physical demands of running can further aggravate these conditions, increasing the risk of injury or complications. Pregnant athletes should work closely with their healthcare providers to manage any existing health issues and adjust their exercise routine accordingly to minimize risks.

The Impact of the Stages of Pregnancy on Running

Let's progress to the impact of pregnancy from conception until birth, taking a close look at research conducted by L'Heveder et al. (2022) on the implications of pregnancy for elite sportswomen.

First Trimester

The initial trimester, a period of rapid fetal development and hormonal shifts, raises concerns about miscarriage risk associated with exercise. However, research brings reassuring news: regular physical activity, including running, doesn't heighten the risk of miscarriage. It may even provide protective benefits, easing mothers' worries about maintaining their active lifestyles early in pregnancy.

Second and Third Trimesters

As we progress into the later stages, the impact of exercise on fetal growth and maternal well-being becomes increasingly relevant. Studies illuminate that consistent physical activity during this period is linked to healthier fetal growth and birth weights. Moreover, moderate-intensity exercises like running can enhance blood flow to the baby, promoting optimal development in the womb.

Intrapartum Considerations

Maternal activity levels shape the birthing experience. As labor and delivery draw near, Evidence suggests that regular exercise throughout pregnancy may shorten labor duration and decrease the likelihood of cesarean section. Maintaining an active lifestyle is also associated with a lower risk of preterm birth.

Postnatal Implications

The benefits of exercise extend beyond pregnancy, impacting postpartum well-being for both mothers and infants. Engaging in physical activity during pregnancy has been shown to reduce the risk of postpartum depression. Remember, it has been stated earlier that exercise releases the "feel-good hormone." Furthermore, exercises targeting pelvic floor muscles can help prevent postnatal issues like incontinence. Recovery will most likely be faster.

It's important that pregnant runners understand what their body goes through in the various stages of pregnancy. Understanding these changes empowers women to stay healthy and keep running as their bodies go through these natural stages.

Catherine Ndereba's Marathon Victories and Global Influence

Catherine Ndereba, born in Kenya on July 21, 1972, didn't just run races; she conquered them. Her story is one of starting small but dreaming big, and her journey to greatness is nothing short of extraordinary. Despite facing obstacles, including the pressures of pursuing a career in teaching, her passion for running made her outstanding.

When Catherine Ndereba was just 12 years old, she fell in love with running. Her dad, who also loved to run, inspired her to try it. Plus, she liked the idea of winning prizes like pencils and books for being the fastest in her physical education class. She became so passionate about running that her classmates started calling her "Crazy Ndereba" because she'd wake up early to run before school and train again after classes. But all that hard work paid off when she became one of Kenya's top athletes, showing her talent on the global stage at the IAAF World Championships in Paris Saint-Denis.

Ndereba's breakthrough moment came when she shattered the world record for the women's marathon, just 6 days after Japanese runner Naoko Takahashi achieved a historic feat by breaking the elusive 2-hour, 20-minute barrier. Ndereba's extraordinary performance, clocking an astonishing 2 hours, 18 minutes, and 47 seconds, cemented her status as an undisputed champion in the world of marathon running.

Among her many accolades, Ndereba's legacy shines brightest at the Boston Marathon, where she claimed victory unmatched four solid times. Her mastery of the challenging course and ability to overcome adversity made her a beloved figure in the running community, earning her the nickname "Catherine the Great."

Catherine Ndereba's Legacy and Influence on Female Athletes

Catherine Ndereba's influence extends far beyond the borders of Kenya. She inspires runners around the world with her remarkable achievements and pure dedication to the sport of marathon running.

In her homeland of Kenya, Ndereba is cherished as a national hero in athletics. Her exceptional talent and numerous accomplishments have inspired generations of Kenyan athletes to pursue their dreams fearlessly and strive for excellence.

One prime example of Ndereba's influence is Ruth Chepng'etich, a rising star in marathon running. Chepng'etich credits Ndereba as her inspiration for pursuing a career in athletics. Like Ndereba, Chepng'etich hails from Kenya and was inspired by Ndereba's achievements to follow in her footsteps. She could emulate Ndereba's work ethic, determination, and success. That helped Chepng'etich greatly in achieving remarkable feats of her own, including winning prestigious marathons and earning accolades on the global stage.

Lessons From the Track

Allyson Felix and Catherine Ndereba are two of the greatest athletes in their sports, but their stories go beyond their incredible achievements on the track. Their journeys teach us valuable lessons about coping with change, never hesitating to advocate for other women's rights, and the importance of perseverance.

Change is a part of life, and how we deal with it can shape our future. Allyson Felix, one of the most successful track and field athletes, faced a major change when she became a mother. Her pregnancy brought new challenges, including fighting for fair treatment of pregnant athletes.

She also took a bold stand against Nike when they didn't support her during her pregnancy. Instead of giving up, she refused to back down from this challenge and started her shoe company, Saysh, which designs shoes specifically for women. This move helped her and created opportunities for other female athletes.

Catherine Ndereba's story also shows the power of embracing change. She started as a promising student-athlete who wanted to be a teacher but shifted her focus to running full-time. Leaving her government job in 1995 to represent Kenya in international races was a big change, but it made her one of the greatest marathon runners in history.

Like these two powerful women, you experience change almost every day. It is important to see such a challenge as an opportunity to grow and become the best version of yourself.

Felix and Ndereba have used their platforms to advocate for important causes, showing how powerful it can be to stand up for your beliefs. Allyson Felix's fight for maternity rights in sports brought major changes. Her public stand against Nike's policies for pregnant athletes made headlines and led to better treatment for all female athletes. Ndereba's success in a male-dominated sport has inspired many young girls in Kenya and worldwide to pursue their dreams in athletics.

Advocacy can create positive change. Never hesitate to speak up for what you believe in as a woman. That way, you can be a great influence in the world of sports.

Another great lesson from these women is the power of perseverance. They trained tirelessly, overcame injuries, and pushed through setbacks to achieve greatness. Felix, despite facing a life-threatening pregnancy complication, continued to compete and break records, becoming the most decorated female track and field athlete in Olympic history. Ndereba, nicknamed "Catherine the Great," won multiple World Championships and Olympic medals and set record-breaking times, all thanks to her unwavering dedication and hard work.

To become outstanding as a runner, you must put in more effort on the training ground. Push yourself beyond the boundaries of your mind. If other women could achieve such a great feat, you can achieve even greater no matter how tough the road may be. The journey of a runner is a story of constant adaptation and evolution. From the first steps to the finish line, every run will teach you something new. You must learn to listen to your body, push through tough times, and enjoy the moments when everything feels just right.

In the next chapter, you will learn about the unique experiences of women runners. You will understand how they adjust their running routines and strategies as they go through different stages of life, from young adulthood to middle age and beyond. I will also show you how successful women runners often balance their passion for running with other responsibilities like careers and family life.

Chapter 5:

Running Through Life

In a country where only men are encouraged, one must be one's own inspiration. —Tegla Loroupe

For many women, running is not just a sport or a hobby; it is a lifelong companion, a source of strength, and proof of personal growth and perseverance. The female runner's path is particularly unique, intersecting with the roles and responsibilities that society often places on women. From balancing careers and families to overcoming societal expectations and personal challenges, the journey of every female runner requires strength and wisdom to keep up.

One of the core focuses of this chapter is the remarkable adaptability and resilience that female runners demonstrate. Life is full of unexpected turns, and the ability to navigate these changes while maintaining a passion for running is truly inspiring. I will share stories of women who have continued to run through several stages of their lives, managed to find time for their passion amidst demanding careers, and even those who have come back stronger after injuries or setbacks.

Adapting Running Through Life's Stages

As women progress through different stages of life, their relationship with running evolves, influenced by changes in their bodies, life circumstances, and even personal goals.

One change that particularly stands out is how a woman's body modifies her running career. Every accomplished female runner, especially those who have been sprinting since they were barely teenagers, can testify to the drastic changes and struggles they encountered while growing up. However, every female runner must come to terms with acceptance. You cannot stop the change that must occur within you because it is a part of normal female physiology. Rather, you must see it as an avenue to reflect on your strengths and weaknesses and gain new drive to build mental and physical strength.

Every female runner experiences growth spurts during adolescence. Her legs grow longer, and her body weight naturally increases due to the distribution of fat around her upper and lower body. Research has shown that the fat distribution on a female runner's lower body can shift her center of gravity and change her gait mechanics. This shift might result in muscle imbalances and overuse injuries, requiring young runners to adapt their training and conditioning routines to prevent and manage these issues.

As women transition into adulthood, hormonal fluctuations, pregnancies, and other physiological changes further influence their running. For instance, as we examined in the previous chapter, pregnancy can temporarily alter a woman's running routine due to increased weight and changes in biomechanics. However, many women find that they can continue running during pregnancy with appropriate adjustments and resume more intense training postpartum.

Aging brings its own set of challenges and adaptations for women runners. At the cellular level, the body's ability to repair and replace tissues reduces with age, meaning recovery times are longer and the risk of injury increases drastically. Without a doubt, she would require fresh training patterns to overcome these challenges posed by aging. She may need to incorporate more rest days, focus on cross-training to maintain overall fitness, and pay closer attention to nutrition and recovery strategies. Adapting and remaining resilient is necessary for women who run throughout their lives. Life stages such as career advancement, motherhood, and menopause require a flexible approach to running. Take menopause, for instance. Women might face weight gain, decreased bone density, and muscle loss during this time. They might need to tweak their routines by adding strength training, taking more rest days, and doing exercises that support bone health to stay active and healthy. These adjustments are key to keeping the joy of running alive throughout their lives.

Deena Kastor's Career Longevity

At 13, Deena Kastor, born on February 14, 1973, in Waltham, Massachusetts, discovered her love for running in the sunny hills of Agoura Hills, California. In no time, she was shattering records and clinching titles, establishing herself as a hero in long-distance running.

Kastor's high school years at Agoura High School were legendary. She dominated the California State Championships, claiming five titles, three state cross-country victories, and two California Interscholastic Federation (CIF) State Meet wins. Her grit and determination were evident as she competed in prestigious events like the Foot Locker Cross-Country Championships and represented her country at international youth games.

Fueled by her passion, Kastor pursued her academic and athletic dreams at the University of Arkansas in 1992. Under the guidance of renowned coach Lance Harter, she blossomed into a track and field star. Endless hours of training and dedication paid off as she clinched four SEC titles and earned multiple All-American honors. Kastor's achievements earned her a spot in the Arkansas Sports Hall of Honor, where she was hailed as one of the state's most decorated athletes.

Deena Kastor's incredible running skills were clear as she won eight National Championships in cross-country. But she didn't just shine in the US. She set American records in the marathon, half-marathon, 5-K, 8-K, and 15-K, showing her amazing endurance across different distances. Her outstanding achievements led Track and Field News magazine to name her the top women's marathoner in the world in 2006.

A major highlight of Kastor's career came in 2004 at the Athens Olympics when she won the bronze medal in the marathon. This was a big deal because she was the first American woman in 20 years to win a medal in this event, marking a comeback for American women's distance running on the world stage.

Deena Kastor's Incredible Resilience and the Bee-Sting Incident

Deena Kastor's incredible running career is filled with victories and records, but her extraordinary resilience truly sets her apart. One of the most unforgettable examples of her tenacity occurred at the 2000 World Cross-Country Championships in Vilamoura, Portugal.

During the 8,000-meter race, something bizarre and potentially dangerous happened: a bee flew into Kastor's mouth and stung the back of her throat. As her throat began to swell, breathing became increasingly difficult. Despite this, Kastor kept pace with the leading runners. The swelling soon became so severe that her airway started to close, and she blacked out.

Amazingly, Kastor regained consciousness and continued the race. Where most people would have stopped, she pushed through the pain and discomfort. Despite the swelling and struggling to breathe, Kastor finished in 12th place. This incredible feat showcased her physical toughness and mental determination.

The bee sting incident is one of the key moments in Kastor's career, showing her toughness and determination. It proved that she could face unexpected challenges and keep going, no matter how hard things got. Her tenacity during that race impressed the running community and sports fans worldwide.

Deena Kastor's Success, the Toll It Took, and Her New Perspective

One of the most impressive things about Deena Kastor's career is how long she stayed at the top. Excelling in a demanding sport like long-distance running for so many years takes smart planning, adaptability, and a keen awareness of your body. Kastor's training and racing strategies provide great examples of how she managed to maintain her elite performance over such an extended period.

Like many others, Deena Kastor's journey as a runner began with uncertainty about her potential. But as she started winning races, she discovered her talent and realized that winning brought joy and approval from others. This fueled her determination to win at any cost, leading her to adopt an aggressive racing style from the get-go.

However, this relentless pursuit of victory took its toll on Kastor. The fear of losing drove her to push herself even harder, almost to the point of burnout. The pressure to constantly win left her feeling frustrated and negative, so she considered quitting the sport altogether.

With the right counsel from her very observant coach, Deena Kastor's mindset shifted when she began appreciating every aspect of her life, including the tough times and the moments of victory. Instead of dwelling on setbacks, she saw them as opportunities to learn and grow. She also found joy in training alongside some of the world's best runners, seeing it as an honor rather than a challenge.

This change in perspective brought a sense of lightness to Kastor's life—a feeling of ease and happiness that she hadn't felt before. By embracing gratitude, she approached running with a newfound joy and fulfillment, free from the pressure to always win. This shift allowed her to unlock her full potential and truly enjoy her journey as an athlete. She unlocked a new level of energy surge when running and made even greater achievements.

Tegla Loroupe's Transition From Competition to Humanitarian Work

Born on May 9, 1973, in Kutomwony, Kenya, Tegla Loroupe grew up in a large family with 25 siblings. Her childhood required her to take on adult roles at an early age. She helped diligently and tirelessly with house chores and cared for her brothers and sisters like they were her children. Despite these challenges, Loroupe's determination was evident early on. Her love for running pushed her to race about 10 kilometers every day with older children, beating them hands down.

Recognizing her running talent, Loroupe dreamed of becoming a professional athlete despite having very little knowledge of what the sport entailed. Her father was so skeptical about her newfound passion, doubting that sports could provide a viable career for her. But Loroupe persisted, driven by her passion for running. In 1989, Loroupe took a significant step forward by competing in the IAAF World Junior Cross-Country Championships, finishing 28th. This was impressive, especially since Kenyan officials initially thought she was too frail to succeed.

In 1994, Tegla Loroupe made history by winning her first major marathon in New York. She was the first African woman to achieve this, becoming an important role model for athletes everywhere and showing that Kenyan women could excel alongside their male counterparts.

After her New York victory, Loroupe continued to shine in marathons worldwide. Between 1997 and 1999, she won three World Half-Marathon Championships. She also earned bronze medals in the 10,000-meter at the World Championships in 1995 and 1999. Loroupe set a world marathon record on April 19, 1998, with a time of 2:20:47 at the Rotterdam Marathon and broke her record the next year with 2:20:43 at the Berlin Marathon. She also held the 1-hour distance world record and world records for running 20, 25, and 30 kilometers.

Marathons were where Loroupe truly excelled. She won the Rotterdam Marathon thrice from 1997 to 1999 and the New York Marathon in 1994 and 1995. Other major wins included the Berlin Marathon in 1999, the London and Rome Marathons in 2000, and the Lausanne Marathon in 2002.

She set world records for 20, 25, and 30 kilometers, won 3 World Half-Marathon Championships, and won marathons in major cities like London, Boston, Rotterdam, Hong Kong, Berlin, and Rome. Loroupe's career shows her incredible talent and determination, making her a true inspiration in long-distance running.

Tegla Loroupe's Humanitarian and Environmental Advocacy

After her successful running career, Loroupe focused on humanitarian work and peacebuilding. In 2003, she founded the Tegla Loroupe Peace Foundation, which promotes peace and development in conflict-prone areas.

One of the foundation's key initiatives is the annual Tegla Loroupe Peace Race. This event brings together warriors from different tribes to compete in a friendly race, fostering mutual respect and understanding. These peace races have significantly reduced violence and encouraged dialogue among rival communities.

Loroupe's humanitarian efforts extend beyond peace races. She strongly advocates for women's rights, education, and environmental sustainability. Her work has earned international recognition, including roles as a United Nations Ambassador of Sport and an advocate for the Sustainable Development Goals (SDGs).

Loroupe has launched various programs to improve access to education, healthcare, and economic opportunities in underserved areas through her foundation. She has also focused on empowering women and promoting gender equality, believing that education and sports can transform lives.

Notable projects include establishing schools in remote areas, providing essential education to children, and organizing health camps that offer medical services to communities with limited access to healthcare. Loroupe also champions environmental conservation, recognizing the vital connection between a healthy environment and community well-being.

Her journey from a young girl running barefoot in Kenya to a global ambassador for peace and development shows what determination and a big heart can achieve. Loroupe's story is a source of inspiration, offering hope to communities working towards peace and progress. Her sports achievements and humanitarian efforts demonstrate how dedication and compassion can create lasting, positive change.

Personal Connection

While I've never considered myself a speedy runner, there was a time when I dreamt of qualifying for and running the prestigious Boston Marathon. It seemed like the ultimate achievement in the running world, the pinnacle every runner aspired to reach. A few years back, I found myself training with some faster friends and noticed a significant improvement in my pace. Encouraged by this progress, I set my sights on qualifying for Boston.

As I embarked on my training journey, I was amazed to see my speed increase. However, despite focusing on hitting qualifying times, I lost the joy of running. Long runs, which used to be my sanctuary, became a constant battle in my mind to go faster rather than relishing the beauty of the trails and roads around me. Despite this, fueled by my stubbornness, I persisted, pushing myself harder and harder to pursue my Boston Marathon dream.

Then came race day, and it turned out to be a disaster. The scorching heat, temperatures soaring to 95 degrees, and the unforgiving blacktop surface made the race challenging. Initially, I felt like I had failed, sinking into a pool of disappointment. But with time, I realized that sacrificing my passion for running for the sake of a race wasn't worth it.

Running has been my constant companion through life's ups and downs, bringing me solace, friendship, and a deep connection with nature. Instead of dwelling on my perceived failure and measuring my worth as a runner based on Boston qualifications, I consciously rediscovered the joy of running. I embraced each run for what it was, focusing on enjoying the journey and listening to my body's cues rather than fixating on pace or comparing myself to others.

I challenge myself in training and trying new things, but I've learned to be confident about meeting specific goals. I've accepted that my running journey is unique to me. It's okay if others have lighter feet than I do. Instead of feeling intimidated, I find motivation in their achievements to keep improving while appreciating my progress and what my body can do.

Lessons From the Field

Running teaches us valuable lessons that apply to life. Just like the trails, life is full of changes. We must adapt and stay strong through every stage. From our first steps to becoming experienced runners, we face different challenges. At first, we're excited and full of energy. But as time goes on, things change. Our bodies change, our responsibilities shift, and our priorities evolve. This is when we need to be adaptable, and adaptability is an exceptional skill that is needed as a runner.

That's only part of the equation; long-term vision and patience are two pillars needed to be successful as a female runner. Think about yourself on a journey with a destination in mind. Long-term vision is like the map that guides you toward that destination, while patience is the fuel that keeps you going, mile after mile, even when the road gets tough.

In other words, having a long-term vision means setting your sights on big goals—like finishing a marathon or achieving a personal best time. This vision serves as your North Star, guiding your training and motivating you to push through challenges.

However, having a vision is only the first step. The real magic happens when you combine it with patience. Running teaches us that progress doesn't happen overnight. It's a gradual journey filled with both highs and lows, setbacks and breakthroughs. Patience is what allows you to weather the storms and keep moving forward, one step at a time.

Think about training for a marathon. You cannot accomplish it in a day or even a week. It takes months of consistent effort, day in and day out, to build the strength and endurance needed to conquer 26.2 miles. Along the way, there will be days when you feel tired, unmotivated, or even sidelined by injury. But it's during these moments of struggle that patience becomes your greatest ally. Instead of giving up, you dig deep, trusting that each small step forward brings you closer to your goal.

Beyond the physical benefits, running also builds mental resilience and emotional strength. It teaches you to stay focused and present, even when your body wants to quit. It shows you that you're capable of more than you ever imagined and that the only limits that exist are the ones you place on yourself.

In addition, the lessons learned from running are lessons for life. They remind us that success is not a sprint—it's a marathon. It's about having the vision to see the bigger picture and the patience to stay the course, even when the road ahead seems long and uncertain. So, as you lace up your shoes and sprint, remember to keep your eyes on the prize, stay patient, and trust in the process. The rewards will be worth it in the end.

As I conclude this chapter, it's necessary to recognize how important it is to understand your body and health to be a successful runner. Running isn't just about pushing through pain or trying to be faster. It's about listening to your body, respecting its signals, and adjusting your training. This mindful approach helps prevent unnecessary setbacks and ensures that running remains a source of joy and fulfillment.

In the next chapter, we'll explore the science that affects female runners. Understanding these factors can help you run better and stay healthy. We'll examine how hormones, body movements, and nutrition impact women's running. With this knowledge, you can adjust your training and lifestyle to meet your running goals. Get ready to run smarter, stronger, and with more confidence.

Sarah Russell's Unbridled Resilience : Women in Running

Review Request Page

"While you, and only you, can move your legs from start to finish, no one runs a marathon alone."

- Alexandra Heminsley, author of <u>Running Like a Girl</u>

Would you help someone like you—curious about the history of women's running and understanding the unique needs of female athletes, but unsure where to begin?

My mission with *Unbridled Resilience: Women in Running* is to share the powerful stories of women who push beyond limits, finding courage and strength in every stride. These stories show the heart, passion, and dedication it takes to be a female runner today.

But to inspire more people, I need your help.

Many readers choose books based on reviews, and your opinion matters! By leaving a review, you can help another woman discover the joy, courage, and resilience found in running. Your review could help...

- One more athlete discover her inner strength.
- One more woman find her passion for the run.
- One more reader feel seen and empowered.

To make a difference, simply scan the QR code below and leave a review:

Thank you from the bottom of my heart!

Best wishes,
Sarah Russell

Chapter 6:

The Science of Running

Each lap is a new chance to show the world what I'm made of. —
Tirunesh Dibaba

The increasing level of participation and continuing improvement in the performance of female runners has made it essential to study the physiology of this group of athletes. This chapter talks about the unique physiological aspects and considerations for female runners, empowering them with a scientific understanding that enhances training, performance, and well-being.

The Female Body in Running

Running changes the human body, and there's no doubt about it. From an increase in endurance to control over your heart's health and body fat composition, running can help you become a fitter, happier, and healthier individual. These impacts can be influenced by certain factors present in the systemic makeup of females, so let's take a look at these unique physiological characteristics.

Hormones

Racing is undoubtedly one of the best lifestyle habits that women can use to support healthy hormones, metabolic health, and likewise mental health. As a female runner, you probably already know that hormones affect your running. However, running also affects our hormones by influencing their synthesis and release. Endorphins are the kind of hormones released when we run, and research has found that the release of endorphins differs with exercise intensity (Parren, 2023).

Moreover, hormonal fluctuations increase when running to deal with the stress on the body. Here, cortisol stimulates glucose release into the bloodstream through insulin regulation, and growth hormone is released to facilitate the adaptation of the muscle to exercise during recovery. For some women, their bodies can react to overtraining by halting their menstrual cycle, thus leading to the shutdown of some physiological processes like reproduction and subsequent impact on the sex hormones like progesterone and estrogen.

How Running Regulates Hormones

Healthy and optimal blood flow enabled by running encourages efficient transportation of hormones around the body, which act as chemical messengers. These balanced hormones enhance your energy level, elevate mood, increase cognitive clarity, and improve your sleep cycle. After recovery from running, the cortisol levels are restored, and a well-balanced nervous system is achieved, which can help in the regulation of hormones.

Hormonal Imbalance Resulting From Running

Running can help improve your hormone level and function, but it can also disrupt them. Overtraining can distort the functionality of your hormones, which can result in anxiety, depression, erratic mood swings, and damage to reproductive health, which are the major symptoms of hormonal imbalance.

A female hormone imbalance refers to the state where a woman's hormones are not at optimal levels, independently or with other hormones in the body (DeCesaris, 2023). Some of the presentations include:

- Low progesterone level, which creates a relatively estrogen dominance state.

- Depressed progesterone and estrogen levels, which are accompanied mostly by anovulation.

- High estrogen level.

Menstrual Cycle

As much as a regular period is a sign of good hormonal and physical health, most women dread their monthly flow. Those few days tend to cause shifts in habits and routines, and the same is true vice versa, as your routines throughout the rest of the month can also affect your menstrual cycle.

As an athlete, you may find that running while menstruating can impact your performance because you may feel a little sluggish while performing your normal routine. This should not come as a shock, considering that hormonal fluctuations can result in cramps, stomach upsets, insomnia, shortness of breath, and elevated heart rate.

Also, confidence level can be affected as a recent survey shows that 54% of women said that they stopped exercising due to their menstrual cycle, and the figure is about 73% in women between the ages of 16 and 24 years old (Carter, 2023).

Can Cramps Stop You From Running?

Most women who experience pain while menstruating know how taunting cramps can be, and even elite athletes are not immune to it. While cramps are certainly horrible, they don't need to ruin your running performance, as exercise itself can help to relieve them. This was proven by Paula Radcliffe in 2002 when she broke the world marathon record in Chicago despite suffering from menstrual cramps in the latter stage of her race.

How Running Changes at Different Points of the Cycle

During the premenstrual stage, declining hormones can cause an inflammatory response that affects sleep, mood, energy levels, and ability to recover. This can lead to a higher risk of injury, as studies have shown that women are more likely to suffer anterior cruciate ligament (ACL) tears than men because of the role estrogen plays in maintaining tissue integrity. Estrogen fluctuations during menstruation increase the risk of ACL injury, and as a study reviewed and published in the Orthopedic Journal of Sports Medicine concludes, the greatest risk is in week two of the cycle (Carter, 2023). When the menstrual flow sets in, energy returns, and hormone levels begin to rise.

Effects of Heavy Menstrual Bleeding

When research scientist and marathon runner Georgie Brunivels surveyed over 1,000 female runners at the London Marathon expo, she discovered that 36% claimed to have heavy menstrual bleeding (HMB) (Carter, 2023). HMB is often associated with anemia, which can result in getting tired easily, rapid heartbeat, loss of energy, and shortness of breath during physical activity. However, most women experiencing HMB supplement with iron, and it was discovered that adjusting iron to a normal level during menstrual flow can have a profound positive impact on performance.

Does Normal Menstruation Affect Your Running?

Anemia resulting from heavy bleeding can be a significant detrimental factor in athlete performance, but a perfectly normal cycle can still affect you negatively if you don't understand and adapt to it properly. Many runners prepare for everything else but menstruation.

Many women might have heard of or taken norethisterone; the period delay drug. This drug contains synthetic progesterone, which is responsible for arresting the shedding of the lining of the womb by keeping up hormone levels. It is a common way of ensuring that the bleeding doesn't arrive at an inconvenient moment, whether it is the marathon day or your wedding day. However, the side effects of this hormonal treatment can end up affecting your performance if you don't prepare your body earlier for it.

Changes in Menstrual Flow

Aside from menstrual flow altering the level of performance of athletes, running can impact a woman's period as some may find shifts in their monthly flow depending on how they train. Professional and long-distance runners sometimes experience inconsistency with their menstrual cycle as a result of their extreme exercise habits. These irregularities are caused by anovulation and hormonal changes resulting in diminished levels of estrogen in the tissues of the uterus and subsequent lack of uterine wall shedding.

Changes in menstrual flow can also result from weight loss. Body fat produces estrogen, which causes the lining of the uterus to build up before it sheds off as monthly bleeding. Weight loss due to caloric reduction or overexercising decreases the amount of estrogen your body produces, causing the lining of your uterus to become thinner.

Without a period for months at a time (leading to reduced levels of estrogen), you are at a greater risk of coming down with stress fractures, osteoporosis, and osteopenia. In addition to weak bones, the immune system can be compromised, leading to frequent sickness in both recreational and professional runners.

Menopause

At different stages of menopause, women experience a significant drop in the level of estrogen. Remember, estrogen plays an important role in maintaining muscles, tendons, strong bones, as well as joints. The stages of menopause include:

- **Perimenopause:** This is the period when women transition into menopause, which can start 10 years earlier, and it is the time during which the estrogen level drops. Symptoms that set in include changes in mood, sleep, hot flashes, sex drive, etc.

- **Menopause:** A woman can be classed in this category when she has not menstruated for a full 12-month cycle. The symptoms experienced are the same as in the perimenopause stage but usually more severe.

- **Post-menopause:** This is the period after menopause. At this stage, the body of the woman has adapted to the low level of estrogen, and the menopause symptoms have decreased.

Effects of Menopause on the Body and How to Mitigate Them

The negative effects of the musculoskeletal system resulting from a drop in estrogen and how female runners can get the most out of their training without injuries will be discussed below:

Effects on Bones

Estrogen plays a crucial role in maintaining bone density and building the framework of bones. The widely known effect of menopause is that a woman becomes more susceptible to bone loss, which can lead to osteoporosis and fracture in extreme cases.

However, weight-bearing exercises can help you build new bone tissues even with the reduced estrogen level. Also, running is a good way of stimulating bone growth in your thigh, pelvis, and legs and can equally slow down the rate of bone loss resulting from menopause. Note that running only enhances the bones of the legs and pelvis. Thus, weight training is encouraged for the stimulation of bone growth in the arms and back.

Effects on Muscles

Low levels of estrogen affect the muscles in four ways:

1. **Decrease in muscle mass:** Menopause affects the quantity of muscle present in your body. Studies have shown that strength training, as well as hormone replacement therapy (HRT), is capable of reversing some of the losses. This is a good reason why you should add strength training to your regular program and adequate dieting to support the training exercises.

2. **Drop in muscle strength and power:** Research has shown that higher levels of estrogen enable muscles to contract better, and these muscles contain more type I (fast twitch) fibers (Louw, 2023).

3. **Prone to muscle damage:** This means that as a result of low levels of estrogen, you tend to get more muscle damage from doing the same exercise when in menopause than when you are younger. To help prevent injuries, adjust the intensity of your training as you go through menopause to allow your muscles to fully recover.

4. **Reduced ability to use fats as the energy source for muscle cells**: The superiority of women in better-utilizing fat for energy production in muscles, unfortunately, changes during menopause. This ability is one of the reasons why women have better muscle endurance than men during low-intensity exercise. It has been suggested that HRT can improve the ability of menopausal women to break down fats.

Effects on Tendons

Tendons are typical strong structures mostly built from collagen fibers. Studies have shown that low estrogen levels can lead to an increase in the breakdown of collagen fibers and slow production of new ones (Louw, 2023). Tendon change can result from a change in the composition of collagen fibers and more reaction to low estrogen, leading to increased healing time when a tendon is strained. This also makes menopausal women more likely to have tendon injuries like gluteal tendinopathy, De Quervian's tenosynovitis, and Achilles tendinopathy.

Effects on Joints

Most joints in the body are synovial joints, which are formed when two bones come together. Strong evidence exists that the drop in estrogen during the perimenopause stage increases the chances at which osteoarthritis develops. Joints, as you know, do not have arteries or veins going through them. They get all their nutrients from the synovial fluids in the joint space.

Increasing estrogen in women susceptible to osteoarthritis has been proven to have positive effects on joint cartilage, muscle, and bone and reduce inflammation of the joints.

Symptoms of Menopause That Affects Running

Every woman's experience of menopause is different, and while some people may notice some difference in their running performance, others may not. However, the following symptoms are likely to affect running:

- **Heavy or irregular bleeding:** Before the menstruation stops, bleeding can often become unpredictable, leading to an increased level of inconvenience.

- **Breast pain:** The breast becomes heavy, tender, and painful.

- **Urinary incontinence:** Urinary incontinence surfaces or can even worsen around menopause and can be aggravated by running.

- **Fatigue:** Unexplainable tiredness sets in with menopause.

- **Lack of motivation:** There is a significant loss in competitive drive to accomplish goals.

- **Pains and aches:** This can be seen before, during, and after running.

- **Weight gain:** The fat composition of the body changes with menopause.

- **Hot flashes:** The body's temperature regulating centers go haywire, making it difficult for runners to control their thermostatic state.

- **Clumsiness:** This can lead to an increased risk of injury.

- **Anxiety:** This can make runners feel less adventurous, resulting from self-doubt.

Mitigating Menopause-Related Changes in Runners

According to Stacy Sims, an exercise physiologist and nutritional scientist, "Menopause does not mean the end of being a competitive athlete" (Warner, 2022, para. 6). Sim's prescription to beat estrogen depletion is described below.

Carefully Lifting Heavy Shifts

Maintaining and preventing the loss of muscle fibers and bones is the key to ensuring that muscle mass is intact. Research conducted by Wendy Kohrt, a professor of geriatric medicine at the University of Colorado Health Center, suggests that those who do resistance training seem to preserve the level of muscle lean mass they had before menopause (Warner, 2022).

CrossFit (a branded fitness program that involves constantly varied functional movements performed at a high intensity) is the best exercise program because it combines both heavy resistance and range of motion exercises. Alternatively, you can add resistance to your preferred training using dumbbells, body weight exercises, and resistance bands.

Replace Endurance Workouts With High-Intensity Interval Training

Resistance training may be the most effective way to maintain muscle mass, but cardio exercises still play an important role in keeping you healthy and strong during the menopausal transition and afterward. These exercises contribute to healthy hearts and lungs, build bone mass, and help burn fats. To get the best of cardio exercises, select high-intensity, calorie-touching interval sessions over slow-distance workouts.

On normal grounds, estrogen naturally prompts your body to synthesize protein into lean muscles. When it is taken away, another stimulus is needed, and high-intensity interval training (HIIT) can do justice to it. HIIT assists your body in building lean muscle mass and also in shrinking fat more effectively than a slow-burn endurance workout. It also helps your body to efficiently produce insulin, making you less prone to insulin resistance, which increases the risk of being overweight and having hypertension.

Change Your Workout Fuel

The reduced level of estrogen causes your body to become more sensitive to insulin and carbohydrates, which can affect your body's metabolism negatively. You may find it difficult to digest fructose-containing sports fuel products. Sims suggests focusing on diets with high-quality fats, proteins, and carbohydrates, which can be obtained from fruits, vegetables, and whole grains (Warner, 2022). Also, consider replacing fructose with simple sugars like dextrose, glucose, and sucrose, which supply menopausal tissues with fewer associated gastrointestinal issues.

Consider Supplements

The National Osteoporosis Foundation recommends a total daily intake of 1,200 milligrams of calcium and between 800 to 1,000 international units (IUs) of vitamin D for maintaining good bone growth (Warner, 2022). It is important to note that a glass of milk contains about 300 milligrams of calcium, and one serving of salmon contains about 250 to 1,000 IUs of vitamin D (wild-caught salmon significantly boosts vitamin D levels). If you feel that you aren't getting enough from your diet, don't hesitate to take a supplement.

You don't need to be an elite athlete to make sure you're staying strong and healthy, but we can draw inspiration from the routines and practices of female athletes like the two we are about to discuss.

Tirunesh Dibaba's Training and Performance

Tirunesh Dibaba, born on June 1, 1985, near Bekoji, Arsi province, Ethiopia, is an Ethiopian distance runner who, at the 2008 Beijing Olympics, became the first woman to win gold in both the 5,000-meter and 10,000-meter races (Lindstrom, 2024). Given the athletic pedigree that runs in her family, it is not surprising that she became a skilled professional athlete. Her cousin Derartu Tulu was the first black woman to secure an Olympic gold medal when she won the 10,000-meter race at the 1992 games. She also won the medal again at the 2000 Olympic Games.

Her sisters, Ejegayehu and Genzebe (older and younger than Dibaba, respectively), are also Olympic and world champions, winning medals across a range of distances. Although Dibaba may have been destined to be an athlete, no one expected that her career would be this great. Her achievements include

- being the youngest female world champion in athletic history.

- being the youngest Ethiopian Olympic medalist.

- being the first female athlete to win both 5,000-meter and 10,000-meter at the Olympics.

- winning six Olympic medals.

- achieving five World Championship victories.

Dibaba's athletic career began in Bekoji, a town near the concentration point of Ethiopia that has produced numerous world-class long-distance runners. She began running when she was in high school until she had the opportunity to start participating in major cross-country races, including her international debut in 2001, at age 15, where she finished 5th. This would later be her entry point into professional running, and although most of her races were track-focused, cross-country was a skill she retained.

Dibaba's Teenage Track Tryo

Dibaba became more grounded in the global spotlight at the 2003 World Athletics Championships in Paris. Dibaba was aged 18 when she took part in her first major international competition. Going straight into the 5,000-meter finals, she overtook her opponents to cross the line in 14:51:72, becoming the youngest female athletic champion in history and the latest in a long line of Ethiopian long-distance greats.

A few months later, Dibaba won the third edition of the Great Ethiopian Run, an event that has become Africa's biggest road race, and its winners are often positioned at the top podium in various global stadiums. For Dibaba, Paris was to be just one of her many world-beating victories as winning five championship golds and six gold Olympics was proof of a glittering athletic career.

Doubling or quadrupling a 10,000-meter distance was not an obstacle for Dibaba, as proven by her professional half-marathon debut in 2012, where she came out victorious. A few years later, Dibaba launched into world marathoning, where she finished in the top three at various editions of the globally recognized races in London and Berlin, as well as the Chicago Marathon in 2017.

How Dibaba Optimized Her Performance Through Understanding Her Body's Needs and Responses

Most determined competitive endurance athletes fail to discover their full performance potential and this is because of their inability to develop their optimal training formula. The most winning endurance athletes are not always more gifted than those who finished a few steps behind them, but because they have found their best way to train and they probably take good advantage of success at all times.

One good way to appreciate how the optimal training formula works is to consider the training methods of famous world champions, and Tirunesh Dibaba is an example of such an athlete. Dibaba trains far more lightly than other world-class runners of her generation, as her longest runs are 80 minutes. She hits the road twice a week, and her short interval sessions range between 150 and 400 meters at a very high speed with short recoveries.

The above formula works for her, and it shows that it is a process that demands your attention to your training and body, with a view to connecting cause and effect so that training patterns that yield poor results will be discarded and good ones retained. It requires that you do the minimum amount of training necessary for you to achieve your goals, or in other words, keep increasing your training volume until you stop improving.

Lessons From the Field

Running affects the physical, mental, and physiological state of a woman, coupled with intermittent events like menstruation and menopause that are capable of aggravating such impacts. Embracing the science of your body as a runner entails understanding the effects of some of the physiological processes on your performance to stay functional all around.

The value of personalization cannot be overemphasized as Tirunesh Dibaba is a typical examples of a world-class runner with training approaches suitable for her body's functionality. However, even with the best scientific understanding and preparation, female runners are susceptible to challenges and adversities, and this will be discussed in the next chapter.

Chapter 7:

Overcoming Adversity

I've never felt that I was less of an athlete or not accomplished athletically because I didn't win an Olympic medal. It's something I would have liked to have added to my resume, but at the same time, I think I can look back at my athletic career and feel that I was one of the best. —Mary Decker

Many women and girls have accomplished so much in the world of sports, from making history to breaking stereotypes and smashing records. While they have excelled, they have also faced many challenges and obstacles along the way compared to their male counterparts. This chapter is a deep dive into the powerful narratives of female runners who have overcome personal hardships and societal obstacles, celebrating their unyielding resilience and spirit.

Personal Challenges and Societal Barriers

Sports science is an ever-evolving field in regards to female athletes. However, women still face lots of challenges capable of impacting their performance. The problems include:

Safety Concerns

Female runners will likely face safety issues while running alone or on isolated pathways during training. You must take appropriate precautions and monitor your surroundings during training. The shocking and tragic death of Ashling Murphy, a runner who was attacked in broad daylight on her local running path, reminds us of the dangers women face. This incident brought some level of attention to the running habits and schedules of most females, including some level of consideration for solo running.

Menstrual Cycles

Menstruation can cause great discomfort and cramps that can affect your performance during running. Your fluctuating hormones can play a factor in your mood as well as how your body reacts to stress during running. It is encouraged that you keep track of your menstrual cycle, observe the patterns of your body concerning your cycle, and note the time of the month when your body feels energized, strong, or tamed. Having proper hygiene products and a suitable plan for managing your periods is the key to making the best of your performance during your period.

Pregnancy

Female runners who are pregnant may face challenges related to the physiological changes in their bodies, which include decreased balance, increased body fluid, and fatigue. It is advisable to consult with a healthcare professional before continuing to run during pregnancy.

Harassment

You can face persistent criticism, unwanted attention, and attack as a female runner, which can be distressing, thus impacting your overall running experience. You must be aware of this challenge and take steps to mitigate it, such as speaking out against molestation and racing in safe areas.

Balancing Responsibilities

Women who balance running with other responsibilities like caregiving, work, family, and household duties may find it difficult to create time for training and participate in races.

Lack of Support

Female runners may not be motivated to compete in races or regularly practice because they lack support from family, friends, and coaches.

Menopause

Several physical changes come with the natural biological process that signifies the end of a woman's reproductive years, and this can bring about functional transformation that can impact performance. These changes, as stated previously, comprise hot flashes, depression, mood swings, fatigue, weight gain, joint stiffness, and decreased muscle mass.

Wage Gap

One of the major challenges that professional female athletes face is the gap in earnings that exists between men and women in sports. This isn't just an issue with athletic sports, as this wage gap exists in almost every sport played by men and women.

Limited Coverage

Part of the reason the wage gap exists between men's and women's sports is that men's sports are more publicized than women's. Money goes where the audience is, and this is why we need to support female athletes by attending their sports events and tuning in to channels where their sports are televised.

Lesser Recognition

Female athletes receive less respect and recognition than their male counterparts. Accomplishments in this field as a female do not look impressive or worth acknowledging, and this can hinder one from getting more opportunities.

Body Negativity

Young adulthood is the most trying time in a woman's life. This is the period when you adjust your personality to fit the status quo, and you are subjected to a societal view of a woman's ideal and desirable body. A female runner might find it difficult to come to terms with the difference in their body and the bodies of women commonly seen as sex symbols.

Women who run, for instance, are not seen with the conventional curvy somatotype common for most ladies. This is because of the continuous rigorous training, which reduces the bulk of calories they take in. A slim and slender body is essential for boosting endurance in long-distance runners because their lesser muscle mass makes them less prone to fatigue.

Mary Decker Slaney's Comeback Stories

Mary Decker has been one of the greatest American track and field middle-distance runners. She was a prodigy who broke the American record indoors when she was only 15 and won Amateur Athletic Union (AAU) titles indoors and out in 1974. Although she has not won an Olympic medal, Decker is recognized as one of the great female runners of her time.

Mary Decker's Journey

Mary Decker was born in New Jersey in 1958 and moved to Huntington Beach, California, with her family by 1969. At age 11, she entered a children's cross-country race, and her easy wins and competition pressure compelled her to keep running. At first, she competed without a coach but still won races for her age group, including a statewide meet.

She later found herself under the guidance of a coach for a local girl's track club, where her natural ability was developed, and within two years, she was breaking records. In 1971, she broke the world record for her age group in the 800-meter race, and her inert desire to win led her to compete in seven races in one week, including a marathon. This led to the emergency appendectomy performed on her, but regardless, she kept pushing herself, training two half hours a day in two workouts.

She qualified for the US Olympic track team in 1972 but was too young to compete then. At age 14, she was recognized nationally when she was allowed to compete in open races unrestricted by her age group. Decker began her career as a professional athlete in international competitions when she was selected to join the AAU's track team in 1973. On the Africa, Europe, and Soviet Union tour, she repeatedly surprised observers with her victories over older athletes. She emerged victorious in the 800-meter in Minsk; by the end of 1974, she held 3 world records for middle-distance races.

However, she became the press subject of international discussion when a runner (Soviet) pushed her off the track during the 4x800-meter relay held in the USSR. Angrily, Decker threw a baton at her opponent twice, which led to the disqualification of both teams. However, her popularity and fame weren't affected. She was dubbed by the press as "Little Mary Decker" as she weighed less than 100 pounds and measured 5 feet in height.

Challenges Mary Decker Faced

In 1975, she had a significant six-inch growth spurt coupled with intensive training sessions, which led to her first deliberate injury that would later impact her athletic career. Physical therapy, anti-inflammatory drugs, and acupuncture were used to treat the shin splint and stress fracture injuries that she sustained. She had to give up her dream of competing in the 1976 Olympic games after the treatment yielded no results.

In 1976, she graduated from high school and relocated to Boulder, Colorado, to enroll at the University of Colorado on a track scholarship despite her ongoing problems with a stress fracture. She successfully underwent surgery for compartment syndrome (a condition where the calf muscles grow larger than the surrounding sheath) in 1977, and she started running without pain after two years. After competing in Australia, she successfully beat her record of 1,000 yards at a U.S. Olympic invitation.

Decker left for college in 1978 to train full-time under the guidance of Olympic medalist Dick Quax. However, she came down with tendonitis, which prevented her from participating in a few events.

Mary Decker's Comeback

After college training, she moved to Oregon, where her career took off again. In January 1980, she set another world record in the US and New Zealand for the 1,500-meter and mile race, respectively, and moved on to break the US record for the 800-meter event at San Diego in February. She qualified for the 1980 Summer Olympics in Moscow but didn't participate due to the U.S. boycott. She competed in other international track meets instead. Her training and competition were on hold for a year following surgery to mend a torn Achilles tendon and shin muscle. Just as before, she made another impressive comeback as she participated in the 10,000-meter race for the first time and beat the previous record by 42 seconds at the European meet in late 1981.

The year 1982 was supposedly her best year, having set five world records in outdoor and indoor games and ran a 4:18 mile. She was named the Female Athlete of the Year by the Associated Press and the International Amateur Athlete of the Year by Jesse Owens. As much as stress fracture continued to afflict her in 1983, it did not prevent her from winning the World Track and Field Championship in Helsinki. That same year, she was awarded the Amateur Sports Woman of the Year from the Women's Sports Foundation and the Sportswoman of the Year by Sports Illustrated.

Mary Decker became the spokeswoman for Nike shoes and equally accepted contracts with Timex and Eastward Kodak in the early 1980s. By 1984, she had held all American distance records from 800 to 10,000 meters. She was a sure bet for a gold medal in the 1984 Los Angeles Olympics, where, unfortunately, she was forced to choose between a 1,500-meter and 3,000-meter race because the events overlapped on the schedule. Decker chose the 3000-meter race and competed with a fan named Zola Budd from South Africa, who was trained to race barefooted on the farm she grew up on.

During the 3000-meter race, the famous collision known to the history of sports occurred when Decker entangled herself with Budd, lost her balance, and displaced a hip muscle. Unable to stand, she was carried off the track, and the only opportunity for a gold Olympic medal was taken away from her. Unfortunately, Budd finished seventh, having to endure the continual disapproving outcry from spectators while Maricica Puica won the race. As to whose fault it was, theories abound, but the inconsolable Decker refused to accept an apology and maintained that she allowed her to take the lead, but she cut across too soon. In an interview by People Weekly in 1994, when asked how she felt about it, Mary Decker said she didn't hate her but rather hated the fact that it was an opportunity that got messed up (*Slaney, Mary Decker (1958—)*, 2024).

Examples of Resilience From Various Female Runners

Bou Samnang: Perseverance That Won the Nation

Bou Samnang is a Cambodian runner who is known for persevering through a race as the last runner, finishing 90 seconds behind the champion, Run Romdoul, in the Southeast Asian Games. Earlier, Samnang was diagnosed with low blood pressure as a result of her chronic anemia during her training in the southwestern Chinese city of Kunming. She was advised to stop running for a while due to this condition, but Samnang insisted that she would participate at the South Asian Games, her first international games, and her coach, Kieng Sarmon, didn't stand in her way.

In the 5,000-meter women's final held in a 60,000-seat stadium, Samnang was among the best regional runners who gathered at the starting line. After the gun sounded and the runners had fallen in position, Samnang found herself in the back of the pack. She was so far behind within some minutes that she was no longer visible to the television coverage. She kept on going even after Onah (an Olympian who eventually won the race), and the rest of the runners finished, not to mention that the sky opened up, and most fans lost their interest.

By the time she finished her race, the stadium floodlights were out, water was already pooling on the tracks, and her uniform was drenched. Runners who finish last tend not to get much praise, especially if they lose by a wide margin, but her perseverance was inspiring, and it won the hearts of many. After the race, her health condition worsened, preventing her from running the 1,500-meter race event as planned, according to her coach (Narin & Ives, 2023).

The video of her determined performance circulated online, and this gave her public praise, including from the Cambodian King and a $10,000 cash award from Prime Minister Hun Sen and his wife. During her interview, she said, "I knew that I would not win, but at the same time, I told myself I should not stop" (Narin & Ives, 2023, para. 4). Her determined finish time illustrated the ideal spirit of sports, and her example will resonate far beyond Southeast Asia.

Edith Masai: A Late Start With a Fast Finish

Stories of runners who discovered talents in sports they never knew about and took up sports late in their lives are surprisingly unique. However, the tale of a Kenyan, Edith Masai, who became the biggest rival in Paul Radcliffe's tomorrow, is remarkable and inspiring.

Masai took up running as a career three years after her ex-husband walked out on her and her little son. Initially, she ran as a means to escape her reality but realized that she was good enough at racing to earn extra cash to supplement her wage as a prison warden. She announced her presence nationally at the top in 2001 when she finished third at the World Cross-Country Championship. In her first Golden League meeting, she did her best and out-sprint the triple world champion Szabo Gabriel in a 5,000-meter race.

At 34 years old, she won the World Cross-Country Championship in Dublin. The day before, Radcliffe won the long race. She had beaten Szabo in a race in Rome the month before.

Radcliffe won against Masai by gaining a psychological edge over her, but she maintains in her statement that "I know that there is much more to come and if it hadn't been for what happened, I would never have realized how good I was at running" (Mackay, 2002, para. 5).

Gabriele Grunewald: Pro Runner, Restless Optimist, and Rare Cancer Advocate

Gabriele Grunewald was a professional American middle-distance runner and a Minnesotan, born and raised in Perham. When she competed for Perham High School, she won a field and single-track state title in the 800 meters. Grunewald moved on to the University of Minnesota cross-country and track and field team in 2004, where she became part of several Big Ten Championship squads. She eventually earned the NCAA Track and Field All-American as a runner-up in the 1,500-meter bout in 2010 (*Gabe Grunewald*, 2024).

Her athletic career highlights include a 4th-place finish in the 2012 U.S. Olympic trials and a championship title in the U.S. indoor 3,000-meter race in 2014. Her best time in the 1,500-meter race was 4:01:48, making her the 11th-fastest performer in U.S. history. Grunewald survived all these bouts with a rare cancer. She was initially diagnosed with a salivary gland cancer called adenoid cystic carcinoma in 2009, followed by thyroid cancer in 2010.

Throughout her cancer journey, she kept on competing and running professionally. She aimed to return to competitions in 2018 and continued training despite setbacks and ongoing treatments. She believed and worked on finding out what was possible regardless of her diagnosis and encouraged other cancer survivors to keep their minds open to achieving their goals by being brave in their own way.

After living with adenoid cystic cancer for 10 years, Grunewald passed away on June 11, 2019, in her home in Minneapolis, surrounded by her family and friends. Her legacy continues with her foundation, Brave Like Gabe, which inspires others to share their struggles while helping to find better and more effective treatments for rare cancers.

Wilma Rudolph: From Disability to Being an Olympic Sprint Champion

Wilma Rudolph, as a young child, was paralyzed by polio, followed by scarlet fever and double pneumonia. Doctors felt she would never walk again, but she believed otherwise. At age 12, she regained the full ability to walk and went further to take up athletics.

At age 16, Rudolph made her Olympic debut at the 1956 Melbourne Games, where she was a member of the American 4x100-meter relay team that claimed a bronze medal. The 1960 Rome games provided the most astonishing moment of her athletic life, as she stormed to gold in the 100-meter, 200-meter, and 4x100-meter relay and broke 3 world records in the process.

The European press named her "Black Gazelle" for her beauty, speed, and grace. Her record-breaking career ended in 1962 with her retirement, after which she devoted herself to coaching and helping underprivileged children. Unfortunately, she died at the age of 54 of a brain tumor.

Lessons From the Field

The stories of these women highlighted the transformative power of adaptability, resilience, and a positive mindset. Their journey inspires young women and reminds them that with passion and determination, their challenges and barriers can be overcome to create an inclusive world for their personalities.

However, while individual resilience is paramount, the support and solidarity from a community can be a great force in overcoming adversity. The next chapter explores the role of community networks and support systems in uplifting and empowering runners through shared experiences and collective strength.

Chapter 8:

The Power of Community

My training is always enhanced when I share it. —Shalane Flanagan

It is no longer news that adversities are bound to be encountered while trying to build and sustain any course; that is why creating your support system is as important as embarking on the journey in the first place because your support system will affect how adversity takes its toll on you.

As seen in the previous chapter, women encountered biological, social, and economic adversities, some of which were, and are still, unavoidable. So, the best approach is to learn how to effectively and efficiently live with adversities and thrive despite them. Focusing on emulating only how the likes of petite Mary Decker or other runners trained and broke their way through may not be enough because not getting fruitful results from modeling yourself after them may frustrate you to the point of wondering if their stories are actually true or perhaps, an ultimate secret ingredient is being withheld. Whatever they have achieved is beyond the number of hours they trained.

Well, hear it again that there are no shortcuts. However, there are easier paths to attaining great heights—or maybe great lengths in this case. Building a community is at the top of the list. As cliché as it may sound, if you truly wish to go far, do not go alone. I mentioned at the beginning of this book how interacting and networking with my fellow sportswomen influenced a significant part of my drive to write this book. If I didn't understand the importance of building, belonging to, or interacting with a community, I may not have had enough motivation to do this. As a matter of fact, interacting with others helps you to identify and familiarize yourself with your strengths and fights because everyone has different and unique struggles. Imagine being on the verge of giving up on a running course because of some hormonal imbalance, and boom, you meet a fellow sportswoman who has not only had the same challenge but overcame or managed it properly and never had to give up on her athletic dreams.

Whatever you do as a running enthusiast—especially a female runner—do not underestimate the role running clubs and other networks have to play in your life.

The Role of Running Clubs and Networks

Running clubs and networks serve as invaluable communities for runners. They foster the spirit of camaraderie and offer motivation and a sense of belonging to their members. These systems provide a platform for runners to connect, share expertise and experience, and participate in group activities that enrich the running experience and promote physical and mental well-being.

What Are Running Clubs?

Running clubs are exactly what they sound like. They are organizations for people interested in running. Each club has different rules and activities, but they're all bound together by the idea that a community is stronger than an individual, so the ultimate goal remains to achieve a collective win through individual wins.

Although running is often perceived as a solo sport, working with a group helps you to stay motivated on your low moments and on days you may be feeling under the weather. Running clubs have continued to grow in their numbers as many athletes have continued to see its significance in their sports life as both rookies and pros.

Depending on a club's integral mission, it can offer a variety of benefits. While some offer physical support, others may be more invested in mental or emotional support, and so on.

During an interview, a member of a running club in Tucson, Arizona, who had run solo for fourteen years before joining the club, had this to say (Schwartz, 2023):

> I had already been a runner for 14 years when I joined the Fleet Feet running club in Tucson, Arizona, and it changed the way I thought about running. I thought I knew a lot about running, but I had no idea what I had been missing. The Tucson group expanded my running world in ways I didn't expect, and they guided me through my first half-marathon and full marathon. You are far more likely to show up and stick to your commitment if you have a training plan, a coach, and teammates. (para. 1-2)

So you can see that even people who eventually join running clubs after taking running as a solitary sport for several years always admit that they had a different and beautiful encounter upon joining these clubs.

Benefits of Joining Running Clubs

Running clubs are resourceful communities that offer a wide range of benefits to their members. Beyond the basic benefits such as providing a platform for running, they also serve as hubs for social interaction, emotional support, as well as personal and professional development. Through these running clubs, individuals gain access to a network of fellow enthusiasts who share their passion for the sport.

Additionally, running clubs often provide well-organized training programs, expert coaching, and access to valuable resources like group workouts, nutrition advice, and injury prevention or management tips. These offerings not only help members improve their running performance but also contribute to their overall health and well-being.

Essentially, running clubs offer much more than just a means to stay active. They provide a supportive environment where individuals can grow, learn, and thrive both as runners and as part of a vibrant community. Here is a more detailed list of the benefits of a running club.

Being Able to Call Yourself a Runner

Due to the sense of belonging that comes with being a member of any club, as a runner belonging to a running club, it becomes easier to identify yourself as one because of your interaction in a community of like-minded enthusiasts who share a common passion for running. By participating in group activities, training sessions, and events alongside fellow club members, it becomes easier for you to adopt the identity of a runner.

The structured nature of many running clubs also gives members opportunities to set and achieve certain goals, whether it's completing a certain distance, enhancing their speed, etc. These series of accomplished milestones within the club help you to develop a sense of ownership over your identity as a runner.

Running Friendship and Camaraderie

Joining running clubs creates opportunities for forming running friendships and fostering camaraderie due to the shared experiences and mutual support within the community.

One of the major things being part of a running club does is that it exposes you to a diverse group of people who share a common interest in running. Through group runs, training sessions, and races, members have the chance to interact with one another, bond over their shared passion, and build genuine friendships based on mutual interests and goals. Members often motivate and challenge each other to push beyond their limits, leading to a supportive and uplifting atmosphere where everyone feels valued and empowered. So, joining a running club not only provides opportunities for improving fitness but also facilitates the formation of meaningful running friendships and promotes a strong sense of camaraderie among members, enriching the overall running experience.

Greater Competitive Edge

Joining running clubs can provide a greater competitive edge, courtesy of several practices common with running communities and clubs, such as:

1. Structured training often includes interval workouts, speed drills, long runs, and strength training sessions designed to improve performance and increase competitiveness.

2. The motivation and accountability that come with being part of a running club help maintain consistency in training, which is crucial for improving performance and staying competitive.

3. Access to resources provided by running clubs, such as expert coaching, training plans, and valuable advice, usually helps members optimize their training and develop effective strategies for competition.

4. Running clubs provide networking opportunities with other runners, coaches, and experts in the running community. These connections can lead to valuable insights, training tips, and opportunities for growth and development as a competitive runner.

Local Running Knowledge

One of the blessings that come with joining running clubs is access to local running knowledge. This is possible when you get to tap into the expertise and experience of members who are familiar with the area's terrain and routes. Usually, members of running clubs tend to have extensive knowledge of the local running scene, from popular trails to neighborhoods suitable for running. Their hands-on recommendation can go a long way for you.

Overall, joining a running club provides access to invaluable local running knowledge, allowing members to diversify their running routes, discover new places to run, and enhance their overall running experience with the guidance and support of passionate runners who know the area well. Being part of a running club can also enable you to explore new running routes and discover hidden treasures in your local area.

Coaching Advice

Running clubs offer expert coaching, providing personalized workout schedules, fitness guidance, and strategies to win races.

Experienced coaches affiliated with the club bring a wealth of knowledge to help you excel in your running journey.

Therefore, joining a running club plays a vital role in guiding and empowering runners to reach their full potential, as it provides access to coaching advice and support from experienced coaches who are dedicated to helping members improve their running performances.

Let's take a look at two popular figures who understood the importance of community and have been able to share their experiences about it.

Shalane Flanagan

As one of the most accomplished distance runners in U.S. history, Shalane Flanagan is best known to be a symbol of endurance and excellence. Her victory at the New York City Marathon remains a prideful accomplishment.

Flanagan's long and noteworthy running career included 16 USATF National Championships, 15 All-American honors, 3 NCAA titles, a World XC bronze medal, and even an Olympic Silver Medal. She set 7 national records during her time, made 4 Olympic teams, and won the New York City Marathon in 2017. She remained at the peak of U.S. distance running for nearly two decades.

As a coach, Flanagan has taken a special interest and commitment in training and mentoring young people, including teenagers. She is dedicated to the cause of amplifying women's running and affording younger athletes a significant source of inspiration.

Facts About Shalane Flanagan

- In 2017, Flanagan became the first female American New York City Marathon champion in 40 years.

- Flanagan is the third fastest U.S. female marathoner of all time.

- Flanagan holds three long-distance running records. Viz:

  - American record in the 10,000 meters: Flanagan set this record in 2008 with a time of 30:22:22.

  - American record in the 15 kilometers: Flanagan set this record in 2016 with a time of 47:03.

  - American record in the indoor 3,000 meters: Flanagan set this record in 2009 with a time of 8:33:25.

- Flanagan coauthored a best-seller cookbook for athletes with her dietician friend Elyse Kopecky, titled *Run Fast. Cook Fast. Eat Slow.*

- Flanagan is a foster parent. Despite having a son, Jack, she and her husband welcomed twin teenagers into their household a few years ago, both of whom happen to be competitive track athletes themselves. On her experience with foster parenthood, she said it has been one of the more rewarding and challenging adventures she's ever taken on (Snider-McGrath, 2020).

Shalane Flanagan's View on Running Communities

By virtue of her personal experiences and accomplishments, Flanagan embodies the idea that success in women's running is not just about individual talent and hard work. It's also about the collective strength and support provided by the community, which fosters a sense of belonging and inclusivity.

She believes that having a strong support system of fellow runners, coaches, mentors, and fans can greatly enhance an athlete's journey, while the encouragement and motivation provided by the community play a crucial role in pushing athletes to excel and reach their full potential.

In a podcast titled, The Power of Self Talk and Community in Competition, she talks about how her coach pushed her to achieve greater fitness without leaving her totally broken despite being the only female athlete among other male athletes in their club at that time.

Desiree Linden

Despite having to battle with stable health of mind and body due to her challenging thyroid issues, Desiree Linden achieved a historic win at the Boston Marathon in 2018, which was a dream come true for her. This is a testament to her unwavering spirit and tactical prowess.

Despite questioning her ability and wanting to explore a smaller running market when she discovered she hadn't won any marathons at 33, Linden chose to readjust her expectations instead while channeling her energy elsewhere.

Facts About Desiree Linden

- Linden is the first female American to win the Boston Marathon in 33 years. Lisa Larsen Weidenbach from America won the Boston in 1985 before Linden brought America back to the top 33 years later at the 2018 Boston Marathon.

- Linden came in fourth position in the Boston Marathon twice. In 2015 and 2017, Linden ended the Boston Marathon both years in fourth position with a time of 2:25:39 and 2:25:06, respectively.

- Linden fractured her femur. Despite her stress fracture in 2012, Linden healed through and made an amazing comeback at the 2016 Rio De Janeiro Olympics, where she qualified in seventh place.

- Linden is a business owner. Apart from being a professional runner, Linden is known to be a persevering entrepreneur who has worked on many endorsements and partnerships with sports brands. She is also a co-owner of a coffee brand called Linden and True.

- She collects whiskey. Desiree Linden enjoys acquiring bottles of whiskey as a hobby and passion. She appreciates the craftsmanship and enjoys exploring the diverse flavors and styles that the whiskey world has to offer. She has collected over 30 whiskey bottles so far.

- Her dog's name is Boston. It is not clear whether this is intentional or a mere coincidence, but Linden has a dog called Boston. I guess her dog doesn't just chase squirrels; he's also chasing victory alongside his owner in all those Boston races!

Desiree Linden's View on the Spirit of Perseverance and Teamwork

Linden's athletic life has always been adorned with all-round perseverance. She never relented or got discouraged by her injury or health diagnosis. Her love for the running sport left her so invested that whenever she felt like giving up, she would look around and see things that reminded her that she had only just gotten started.

Desiree Linden's reputation for sportsmanship has solidified her as not only an outstanding athlete but also a role model for aspiring runners worldwide. She is respected for her exceptional show of sportsmanship both on and off the track. She is known to have pronounced humility, great respect for her fellow competitors, and graciousness in victory and defeat.

Once, she slowed down to wait for her fellow American runner Shalane Flanagan, who dashed into the mobile toilet to ease herself during the 2018 Boston Marathon, and they both later caught back up. This singular act exemplified Linden's selflessness and camaraderie within the running community and earned her widespread admiration and respect. Linden never failed to mention how helping Shalane helped her regain her diminishing vigor.

My Life-Changing Experiences

One major thing I have gained from my running journey that I can confidently place over everything else is the importance of community. As an introvert, it hasn't always been easy, but understanding the benefits has helped me explore networking opportunities in my field without putting a lot of pressure on myself.

Remarkably, in February 2017, I took a big leap and showed up to this new running group that was meeting downtown. This was totally out of character for me, but I desperately wanted to share my passion with like-minded people, so I went for it. I may have doubted if a soothsayer told me I'd be meeting lifelong friends that night, as that was the least of my expectations.

What I took as a way of breaking free from my shell turned out to be what would ultimately form and encourage my entire running journey. The leader of that group would go on to become my coach, crew, pacer, and best friend. Without her, none of this would have been possible. The community she created and nurtured helped me to come out fiercely from my shell and learn to thrive with others.

Similarly, back in 2022, I joined another local run club that was founded by another strong and resilient female runner. She intended to build a community of frequent running partners, so she created an informal running group focused on her local area back in March 2021. After a few years, the group had grown to over 1,000 people in the Facebook group and over 100 people showing up weekly, physically, for the group runs.

This group also incorporated fundraising for charities as well as reaching out to other running clubs in the community for joint runs, indoor and outdoor rec soccer teams, cross-training workout days, and so much more.

It's been merely a few years, yet it is incredible to see how far this group has come, and I look forward to seeing what it will become in the future. In this group, I see a family, my biggest cheerleaders, strongest advocates, and greatest encouragement through all walks of life beyond my running pursuit. Through friendship, accountability, and encouragement, this community has shaped me, taught me, and helped me grow tremendously, not just physically but also mentally and emotionally.

Lessons From the Field

It has been evidently elaborated in this chapter how important running communities are in the life of every runner. The truth remains that by sharing your strength with others, you get to strengthen and empower yourself. It is a win-win situation.

Shalane Flanagan and Desiree Linden demonstrated great teaming in running, which is highlighted by their mutual support and camaraderie. Despite being competitors, they demonstrated the power of teamwork and encouragement within the running community.

One key insight was how Linden demonstrated sportsmanship by slowing her pace when Flanagan needed to take a bathroom break mid-race. Also, after the 2017 New York City Marathon, Flanagan credited Linden for inspiring her to push through challenging moments in the race. Flanagan acknowledged Linden's grit and determination, recognizing the importance of having fellow runners as sources of motivation and support.

These stories illustrate how running is not just about individual achievement but also about building connections, fostering team efforts, and supporting one another through both triumphs and setbacks. The running community continues to serve as a source of encouragement, inspiration, and solidarity, enriching the sport and making it more than just a competition but also a shared journey towards personal and collective excellence.

Take a moment to reflect on your own community involvement and the supportive networks you have—or aspire to build—especially on your running journey. Consider the people who have cheered you on during races, offered words of encouragement during tough training sessions, or simply shared the joy of crossing the finish lines with you.

Reflect on the impact these connections have had on you. How have they motivated you to push your limits, overcome obstacles, and celebrate achievements? How can you contribute to fostering a supportive community within your running circles?

Whether it is becoming part of a local running group, volunteering at races, or simply reaching out to fellow runners for support and encouragement, there are numerous ways you can cultivate meaningful connections within the running community. By actively seeking out or building supportive networks, you not only enhance your own running experience but also contribute to the collective spirit of solidarity that makes the running community unique and special.

So, as you lace up your running shoes once more to hit the track or the trails, don't fail to recognize the power of a community in propelling you forward on your journey. Embrace the connections, share in the triumphs and challenges, and together, let's continue to inspire and uplift each other every step of the way.

Conclusively, as you seek new challenges and push limits in your running venture, the support and inspiration of a community become even more crucial and, at a point, indispensable. Acknowledging this will help you get to and remain at the top.

Chapter 9:

The Ultradistance

I expect myself to give it everything I have in a race, and that's about where the expectations end. —Courtney Dauwalter

Ultramarathon, which used to be a niche sport, has become a widely practiced athletic game throughout the past decade. It is so different from a traditional marathon because it does not have many requirements and does not follow the general rule of marathon running that says, "the flatter the course, the better." This chapter explores ultrarunning, a realm that tests the limits of human endurance and spirit. It's designed to immerse the reader in the awe-inspiring journeys of ultrarunners, revealing how they push beyond conventional boundaries and what drives them to keep moving forward, mile after mile.

The Allure and Challenges Of Ultrarunning

Ultrarunning, also known as ultramarathon, is a foot race event or challenge that covers a distance longer than 26.2 miles or 42.195 kilometers. It can be run on or off the road or both, and race distances commonly start at 50 kilometers (31 miles), 50 miles, 100 kilometers (62 miles), or 100 miles.

Stage Races

Many of the ultramarathons that reach distances over 100 miles are multi-day races and are regarded as "stage races." In this kind of ultradistance racing, there are prescribed distances (or stages) an athlete must run daily. Each stage tends to finish where the runner will spend the night, and it could be a self-sufficient camp or a higher-class space like a luxury accommodation.

Famous ultramarathon stage races include:

- The Everest Trail Race (105.6 Miles)

- RacingThePlanet for Desert Race Series (155.3 Miles)

- The Trans Atlas Marathon (100 Miles)

- The Marathon de Sables (157.8 Miles)

- Dragon's Back Race (186 Miles).

Common Ultramarathon Traits

Ultramarathon Terrain

While a typical marathon is mostly on a road, your standard ultradistance race will be run in nature, which includes mountain plains, forest trails, or deserts. This implies that the underfoot might be challenging, and thus, you might have to use all four limbs (hands and legs) to lift yourself over obstacles, like bouldering.

Oftentimes, the course of an ultramarathon race consists of a significant amount of elevation gain, which means that most ultrarunners' racing preparation is spent on hilly surfaces. However, there is no single-fit size description of an ultramarathon terrain because there are many races of the same kind that are completely flat and on the tarmac. An example is the Berlin 100-mile marathon, which follows the paved length of the old Berlin Wall.

Aid Stations

Aid Stations are the supply checkpoints on the routes of an ultramarathon race, which provide runners with food, hydration, and medical personnel for emergency cases. The supplies can be as basic as a bottle of water and some sweets or mints, but they are still anticipatory points during an ultramarathon. Also, it is common among ultrarunners to break up their distance psychologically into more manageable periods using aid stations. For instance, if there are 10 aid stations positioned every 10 miles in a 100-mile race, it becomes a good strategy for a runner to think 10 miles ahead.

Support Crew

Most ultradistance races, especially the longer ones, allow runners to come along with a support group on race day. This support crew is a trusted team of race-day helpers who can be running buddies, friends, or family.

The role of a support crew is to provide both moral and physical support to their runners. This support ranges from preempting when the runner may be hungry to indicating when their bottles need to be refilled.

Pacers

Pacers are a dedicated team of runners that run alongside ultrarunners during a chunk of their race time to keep them on track while running. For example, they are often found during the time they know that a runner might experience some struggles, like the 3 a.m. shift during a 100 miler.

As a standard ultrarunner, a pacer might be the difference between finishing and dropping out, while elite ultrarunners might have a pacer to hit a particular running speed that they want to achieve.

Effects Of Ultrarunning On Your Body

- **Stomach:** One of the challenges ultrarunners face during long races is always food-related. When you cover big distances, you inevitably have to eat as you continue to run, or you will be out of energy and crash. Thus, during ultramarathons, aid stations offer a wide variety of foods ranging from sandwiches to fruit. However, eating while you run can result in gastrointestinal issues. This is because your body does not make digestion a priority while you run, leading to your circulatory system diverting away from the tissues of your stomach to your muscles to keep them more active.

- **Feet:** With the challenging conditions and terrains of ultras—mud, sand, rain, etc.—as well as the number of hours spent on the trails, runners are susceptible to developing blisters. Most ultrarunners have made several attempts to mitigate this, from wearing toe socks to investing in wide-toe shoes, but even then, blisters are sometimes inevitable.

- **Eyes:** Ultrarunning can cause blurred or reduced vision if held in dry or windy conditions because the cells responsible for producing the protective liquid in the eye can get damaged due to low humidity.

- **Mind:** During ultramarathon training, runners tend to build up their mental strength alongside their physical endurance as it is a tough pursuit. During ultradistance races, an athlete may have to dig into the mental reserve they built during training.

It is also common for ultrarunners to experience hallucinations while running, and to many, it is the fun in it. Courtney Dauwalter, an ultramarathon champion, in an interview about her hallucination while running, said that one time she was running along and next to the trail was a colonial-looking woman churning butter. She was there, but it wasn't real (Andrews, 2022).

Why People May Want To Participate In Ultramarathon

Motivation is personal and differs from one runner to another. It is a drive that sees ultramarathon as something intrinsically rewarding, a way to seek limits, and a way to have an experience of adventure in nature. Here are some of the reasons why people run ultramarathon.

Intrinsic Motivation

Some runners participate in ultramarathons just to prove that they can run such a long distance. Intrinsic reasons can be one of the major motivators inspiring runners to withstand the agony of such a distance, especially when they compete in several competitions. As for experienced runners, they are rewarded and inspired by the experience of the race itself, not by the admiration or results of others.

Seeking Limits

Most ultramarathoners want to find their limits, and once they do, they want to go beyond them. It lies in long-distance runners to challenge their bodies and minds. Coping with difficulties, mental loss, exhaustion, and the fear of dropping out of the race is part of the experience, and it is appreciated by most runners. If they finish, regardless of the difficulty, the contentment and happiness are greater.

Finding Tranquility Through Meditation

Running can be a state of meditation as it helps the mind become clear and tranquil (a state of being calm). Most runners can testify to the meditative role of a short jog in the woods, and this experience is said to become more intense as the distance gets longer.

Once an ultrarunner is out for a day or longer, her mind has plenty of time to ponder certain questions about life or why an ultramarathon was chosen. Also, the silence of nature provides a conducive environment for meditation.

The Movement

Deeply rooted in evolution, humans have been running since the beginning of time, and this is because it involves simple movements. Ultramarathoners love this movement because it adds speed, allowing nature to be seen in a shorter time and yet slow enough to allow one to pay attention to the surroundings.

This experience cannot be found with skiing or biking because more attention is paid to the technique, and the speed is too high to enjoy the mountains.

Experiencing Nature

The experience of ultrarunning in nature is about the weather, mountains, and the lights. An ultramarathon is a way to fully explore the vast, beautiful natural world. It is a stunning experience to be caught in a snowstorm one night and see a clear sunrise the following morning.

The Adventure

Running an ultramarathon is taking a journey, and when you are on the trail for 24 hours or more, you experience lots of unpredictable environmental happenings.

Changing weather, strange responses of the mind and body to stress, and the instances where things may go wrong can make an ultramarathon an adventure.

Addiction

Addiction is not motivation, but it can have the same function. Certain ultrarunners can get addicted to this sport because of the flow, meditative moments, adventures, as well as the highs and lows of the terrains.

Courtney Dauwalter's Ultra Achievements and Mindset

Courtney Dauwalter is an ultrarunner known for having lots of fun while participating in extremely long races. In most of her 100-mile ultradistance trail races, she is often seen smiling, laughing, and in much better condition than other typical runners or her elite-level rivals. While ultramarathons are races exceeding 26.2 miles, Dauwalter's achievements tend to take place at distances between 100 and 250 miles (Foster, 2023).

Courtney Dauwalter's Achievements

At 38 years old, Dauwalter's lists of achievements are shockingly interminable as she is a 4-time holder of Ultra Running Magazine's Ultrarunner of the Year. She has held multiple course records for extremely long races around the US and abroad. Dauwalter's breakout moment came at the 2017 edition of an annual 240-mile race known as Moab 240 held in Utah. She showed her interest in participating in the race shortly after deciding to be a full-time ultrarunner, and Dauwalter unbelievably completed the course 10 hours ahead of other competitors.

She had obliterated the women's course record by more than an hour and had finished the race in the 23rd fastest time in the 45-year history of the race. Also, she won the Ultra-Trail du Mont Blanc (UTMB), a 172-kilometer ultrarunning race around Mont Blanc Massif in Chamonix, France. Although she had won the race twice before, her running strategy around the 106-mile loop that passed through France, Switzerland, and Italy with 33,000 feet of elevation gain was impressive.

Growing up in Minnesota, Dauwalter was a Nordic skier with four-time state championship titles in high school who competed for the University of Denver while in college.

She found her talent in long-distance trail running while living in Golden and working as a high school teacher (Metzler, 2023). But despite her brilliant rise, she admitted that she encountered certain challenges when she moved from 50-mile to 100-mile races 10 years ago.

Courtney Dauwalter has won more than 50 races of 50 kilometers and longer over the past 10 years, which include

- the Madeira Island Ultra Trail, which she won twice with a distance of 115 kilometers.

- the Western States 100 in California.

- the Hardrock 100 in Colorado, where she set the women's course record this year (2024), breaking the previous record also set by Dauwalter last year.

- the Ultra-Trail du Mont Blanc (UTMB) in Europe.

- the Moab 240 in Utah.

- the Big Dog's Backyard Ultra 2020 in Tennessee, where she ran 283 miles over 3 days to win the sole survivor race.

- the Bandera 100-kilometer ultradistance race in Texas.

- the Transgrancanaria 128 kilometer ultramarathon held in The Canary Islands.

Courtney Dauwalter's Approach to Training, Workout, Diet, and Racing

When Dauwalter graduated from college, she started running on her own and never considered hiring a coach because she was just running for fun. At first, she based her training on workouts and methods of previous coaches, and she enjoyed the creativity that came with it. However, instead of writing a weeks-long training plan with specific benchmarks and paces, Dauwalter takes an approach in which each day determines the adventure. In contrast to many athletes who openly share their training routines and progress, Dauwalter is known for her extraordinary secrecy regarding her personal training regimen. However, the pieces of information gathered about her training methods are discussed below.

The Miles She Runs Per Week

While Dauwalter doesn't have a standard number of miles she runs per week, she has, in multiple interviews, said she typically runs 10 to 100 miles per week. In her words, she said "I run every day, some days multiple times a day and sometimes all in one go. I don't follow a plan, but I get 110 miles per week. I just go out and run how my body feels" (Ellis, 2023, para. 5).

Does She Follow a Training Plan?

Dauwalter has made it clear in her interviews that she doesn't follow a strict training plan. Rather, she decides the day's training method and routine after waking up and getting her caffeine fix. She decides her run for the day based on how her body and brain feel. Sometimes, it can be a long run on some of her favorite trails or a day that the hill repeats and intervals, whereas some days can be uncertain until she steps out of the house and allows her feet to choose the routes.

Does She Do Speed Workouts?

Dauwalter does speed workouts sometimes, depending on how she feels. So, in a week, she can be doing multiple speed workouts and hill workouts, but at other times, she isn't doing any at all. This is because her speed workouts are usually not planned out, and she only does them when she finds hills to speed work on along her trail.

Does She Track Her Zone and Heart Rate While Running?

Dauwalter does not follow time-zone-based training plans like the one we have commonly seen. According to her, it is based on feeling guided by her internal zone gauge. She considers her wins as effort-based and does not think of them as her pace, heart rate, or zone.

How Long Are Her Weekly Runs?

It is shocking to know that Dauwalter's normal weekly long run is between three and four hours because she aims for quality over wear and tear on the body. She avoids going into pain caves while training because, according to her, she likes saving them for race day. For instance, before Hardrock 100 in 2022, she did an 8-hour long run, which she considers just spending time in the mountains.

Does She Do Cross-Training?

Cross-training is one of the basic routines she does every day before her run. It targets her cores, glutes, hips, general trunk strength, and mobility.

Is She on Any Specific Diet?

Dauwalter is an ultrarunner who doesn't follow any particular diet. It is common knowledge that she eats healthy all the time and does not deny herself things that she loves. Again, she is an athlete who follows her mindset by listening to her body and making sure that she enjoys life. Like she said, "I eat whatever I want and don't get hung up on planning or counting calories or grams or anything. I just eat whatever my body is craving" (Ellis, 2023).

What Does She Eat While Running?

Like most ultrarunners, Dauwalter has talked about how she handles her nutrition over the years of training. At first, she could eat whatever she thought looked good at the aid station, like pickles and chips, but she has refined her approach as the years go by. In her recent interviews, she discussed how she had switched from common light snacky foods to primarily liquid-based diets consisting of water and liquid calories.

Personal Connection

I never imagined the changes entering the world of ultrarunning would bring into my life. My first ultramarathon was in 2017, a 50-kilometer race event in DeWitt, IL. In these few years, ultramarathons have taught me certain lessons.

Patience

I had to learn that I wasn't going to get it all right the first time, and practice truly does make it better (never perfect). For example, it took me years to figure out my nutrition style during a race. In most of my races, I would hit a seven-hour time limit before my stomach began to rumble and hurt. So it was either I finished in under seven hours (but then I was slow) or figured out what was going wrong. For years, I continued to try different things throughout my ultra training until I finally ran a race and was able to blow past that seven-hour baseline, still feeling strong.

I finally found what worked for me, and it felt amazing to know how hard I had worked to tackle that hurdle.

Paying Attention to Your Body

I have learned also how to listen to my body and the difference between hurting and being hurt. Running an ultramarathon is going to come with some pain. It's inevitable as you are pushing your body past normal limits. But it is important to learn the difference between hurting and being hurt. I had to learn that the frustrating twinge in my foot that hurts was just par for the course, and I could push through; I could maybe change my shoes to switch things up and keep going.

I learned the hard way—because I'm stubborn—that a sharp pain in my knee should not be ignored during a race because the time I adamantly fought through the pain for 20 miles in a race, my knee completely gave out, and this was as a result of a stress fracture. Now, I respect what my body says and also take some time off to heal rather than further injuring myself and causing a longer recovery and potentially permanent damage to my body.

Respect for the Environment

Another thing that ultradistance running has taught me is to respect and care more for the environment. As a road runner for several years with little experience in the woods or trails, the ultramarathon opened my eyes to the beauty of our natural world. I learned how to respect the forests and wildlife by disposing of my trash carefully, staying on the cut paths, and being mindful of the habitat around me so as not to disturb the environment.

I also joined trash pick-up days and trail cleaning days to further protect the beauty of nature. I discovered ways to identify potentially harmful wildlife and plants to protect myself whilst I gave them their space because they were there first.

Lessons From the Field

In all, an ultramarathon is an event that trains one on endurance, mental fortitude, and continuous pursuit of personal best. From this chapter, you can see how the extraordinary feats of ultrarunners are pushing the boundaries of the sport and inspiring a new generation of runners. However, the next chapter will explore the future of women's running, looking into the emerging trends, continued challenges, and the ongoing journey of empowerment and achievement in the sport.

Chapter 10:

Strides Forward

When anyone tells me I can't do anything... I'm just not listening anymore.
—Florence Griffith Joyner

As we look ahead to the future of women's running, there's so much to be excited about. You will be amazed at the new trends emerging in the sport, from innovative training techniques to the latest gear designed specifically for female athletes. I will also shine a spotlight on the ongoing advocacy work supporting women runners, ensuring they have the resources and opportunities to succeed.

The landscape of women's running is also changing in remarkable ways. More women are participating in races than ever before, and there's a growing sense of community among female runners. Events like women's marathons and running clubs are becoming more popular, providing spaces where women can support and motivate each other.

My aim with this chapter is to inspire you. By looking at the possibilities for the future, we want to show how every woman, whether a seasoned athlete or just starting, can be part of this exciting journey. The big goal is to encourage the next generation of female runners to pick up the torch, push boundaries, and continue the progress toward greater inclusion and empowerment in the sport. So, prepare to be motivated and to see how you can be a part of the bright future of women's running.

Women Sprinters Now

In women's sprinting, several female athletes have distinguished themselves as the best in the world. These sprinters break records and inspire future generations with their incredible performances and dedication to the sport. Here are some of the top women sprinters today:

Elaine Thompson-Herah

A dominant force from Jamaica, Thompson-Herah has multiple Olympic gold medals and continues to set new standards in the 100-meter and 200-meter events. As the icing on the cake, she is the second-fastest woman to compete in a 200-meter sprint. Championing the Olympics 5 times, she is also recognized as the fastest 100-meter female sprinter.

Shelly-Ann Fraser-Pryce

Also from Jamaica, Fraser-Pryce is known for her consistent performance and longevity in the sport, which has earned her numerous world titles and Olympic medals. Her most notable award is the Laureus World Sports Award for Sportswoman of the Year in 2023.

Shericka Jackson

Another Jamaican sprint star, Jackson began her career boldly as a 400-meter sprinter. She also excels in both the 100-meter and 200-meter, showcasing her versatility and strength. Her most notable achievements include bagging gold in the 4x100-meter relay at the 2019 World Championships. She has also earned herself a 200-meter sprint Diamond League title.

Sha'Carri Richardson

An American sprinter known for her speed and vibrant personality, Richardson has quickly risen to prominence in the 100-meter. At the 2023 World Championships in Budapest, Sha'Carri Richardson dazzled the world by winning gold in the 100-meter. She also made waves at the Diamond League in Doha, where she clinched her first victory in the 100-meter with a stunning new meeting record of 10.76 seconds despite a slight headwind.

Marie-Josée Ta Lou

Marie-Josée Ta Lou is a renowned sprinter from Cote d'Ivoire who specializes in the 100-meter and 200-meter events. Despite not having won an Olympic gold medal, she is celebrated as one of the best sprinters in the world. Marie-Josée Ta Lou started gaining international attention with her performances in various African championships. Her speed and determination quickly set her apart in the sprinting world.

At the 2017 IAAF World Championships in London, she made a significant impact by winning silver medals in both the 100-meter and 200-meter events. This achievement placed her among the top sprinters globally and showcased her consistency and competitiveness on the world stage. In 2022, Ta Lou set an African record in the 100-meter with an astounding time of 10.72 seconds. This record is proof of her incredible speed and skill, solidifying her status as one of the fastest women in the world.

Aleia Hobbs

An emerging talent from the US, Hobbs has made significant strides in the 100-meter, becoming one of the fastest women in the world. Aleia Hobbs made headlines in February 2023 when she set a North American indoor record for the 60-meter with a blazing time of 6.94 seconds, making her the second-fastest woman ever. Beyond her achievements, Hobbs has also shined on the international stage, winning 3 world medals as a key member of the U.S. women's 4x100-meter relay team.

Julien Alfred

Julien Alfred's achievements on the track are nothing short of spectacular. At the 2022 Commonwealth Games, she sprinted to a silver medal in the 100-meter, showcasing her world-class speed. Indoors, she's equally impressive, holding the North American record for the 60-meter dash. Alfred made history in the NCAA by becoming the first woman to run the 60-meter in under 7 seconds. Beyond these records, she's also a three-time NCAA Division 1 individual champion, cementing her status as a top collegiate athlete.

Dina Asher-Smith

Dina Asher-Smith is blazing fast in 2023. She made a big splash at the 2019 World Championships, taking home gold in the 200-meter, silver in the 100-meter, and silver in the 4x100-meter relay. By 2023, Asher-Smith has racked up 8 national titles in various distances, including the 60-meter, 100-meter, and 200-meter indoors and outdoors. Her incredible speed and versatility make her one of the top sprinters to watch.

Tamari Davis

A young American sprinter with a bright future, Davis is known for her speed and potential to become one of the best. In August 2023, she blazed her way to the World Athletics Championships in Budapest. There, she secured a spot in the 100-meter final and zoomed across the finish line, claiming the 9th position. Talk about speed and skill in action!

Twanisha Terry

Twanisha Terry is a track superstar known for her lightning speed and impressive accomplishments. As part of the U.S. women's 4x100-meter relay teams, she sprinted to victory, grabbing the gold medal at the prestigious 2022 World Athletics Championships. But her talent doesn't stop there. Terry's solo skills shine just as bright, and she clinched an individual NCAA Division 1 title to add to her list of achievements. She's a force to be reckoned with on the track and in the record books.

Predictions and Trends for the Future of Women's Running

Shoes

Exciting changes are underway in the world of women's running, especially when it comes to shoes. Brands are stepping up their game, crafting footwear specifically designed to support women's unique needs. These aren't just smaller versions of men's shoes; they're tailored to fit the female foot and enhance performance.

One big buzzword? Technology. With the help of AI, finding the perfect shoe fit has become easier than ever. By crunching data on things like foot shape and how you run, AI can recommend the ideal shoe, ensuring maximum comfort and performance while reducing the risk of injury. But it's not just about function; it's about sustainability, too. Brands are getting greener, using eco-friendly materials and processes to make shoes that tread lighter on the planet. This is a big win for women runners who care about the environment.

Hormone Therapy

One exciting trend in women's running is the use of hormone therapy, especially among menopausal master-runners. As women age, hormonal changes can affect their running performance and overall health. Hormone therapy involves taking medications containing female hormones to help counteract these changes.

This trend is catching on because menopause can bring challenges like reduced bone density, muscle loss, and changes in energy levels, all of which can impact running. By trying hormone therapy, women hope to see improvements in these areas, potentially boosting their running abilities and overall well-being.

However, it's important to remember that hormone therapy isn't a one-size-fits-all solution and comes with potential risks and side effects. Women interested in hormone therapy should talk to their doctors to see if it's right for them based on their health and medical history. As more studies are done and awareness spreads, hormone therapy could become a valuable option for menopausal runners looking to maintain their love for running and stay healthy.

How These Advancements Will Impact Women's Running

Women's running shoes and hormone therapy trends could shake up the running world in exciting ways, from elite athletes to everyday runners.

Brands are realizing that women's feet have unique needs, starting with shoes. This means elite runners can expect better-fitting, more supportive shoes that could give them an edge in competition. For beginners and hobbyists, comfy shoes designed just for women might make running more enjoyable and help prevent injuries.

Now, onto hormone therapy. Elite runners in the masters category might turn to hormone therapy to combat the effects of aging. If it proves effective, we could see older athletes stay competitive for longer. For everyday runners, hormone therapy could make running more accessible and enjoyable for women experiencing menopause-related challenges.

These trends could revolutionize women's running by providing better gear and new solutions for staying active and competitive at every level.

Ongoing Advocacy and Development in the Sport

Safety Initiatives

Safety is a paramount concern for women runners. Various studies and surveys reveal that most women are apprehensive about their safety while running outdoors. For instance, a survey indicated that 92% of women runners are worried about their safety during outdoor runs (Adidas, 2023). This widespread concern has led to several proactive measures to address the issue.

Adidas, for example, has been at the forefront of campaigns like Ridiculous Run, which aims to raise awareness about the violence and safety challenges women face while running. These campaigns seek to highlight the issue on a larger platform, pushing for societal changes that ensure safer environments for female runners. Furthermore, brands are adopting different approaches to enhance safety. This includes developing innovative safety gear such as reflective clothing and personal alarms and promoting community-based running groups. These groups provide a sense of security through numbers, allowing women to run together and support each other.

Inclusivity in Races and Clubs

Inclusivity in running is essential for creating a welcoming and supportive environment for all runners. Efforts to promote inclusivity focus on breaking down barriers related to race, gender, and socioeconomic status, ensuring that everyone feels valued and included.

Organizations like Ourea Events have implemented comprehensive equality, diversity, and inclusion policies. These policies ensure that their events are accessible and welcoming to a diverse range of participants, reflecting a commitment to inclusivity at the organizational level. Additionally, grassroots initiatives play a crucial role in making running more inclusive. Community efforts often involve local running groups and events that specifically aim to be welcoming to underrepresented groups, providing support and fostering a sense of community.

The running industry also recognizes the importance of inclusivity, with more races and clubs adopting inclusive practices. These efforts include offering diverse running events, promoting diverse representation in marketing materials, and actively reaching out to underrepresented communities. By prioritizing inclusivity, the running community works toward a more equitable and diverse sport.

Pay Equity

The issue of pay equity in sports has garnered significant attention, with advocacy efforts highlighting the need for equal compensation for women athletes. The gender pay gap in sports remains a contentious issue, with women often earning less than their male counterparts despite comparable performance and dedication.

Awareness campaigns are crucial in shedding light on the importance of closing the gender pay gap. Articles and advocacy pieces argue that women athletes deserve fair compensation, emphasizing that pay equity is not just a matter of fairness but respect and recognition for their contributions to the sport. Legal and policy changes are also being pursued to ensure gender pay equity. Some sports organizations have begun to lead the way by offering equal prize money and salaries for men and women, setting a precedent for others to follow.

Gender Equality

Gender equality in running and sports, in general, is a critical area of focus. Ensuring that women have equal opportunities and are treated with the same respect and recognition as men is essential for the growth and development of women's sports.

Books and media play a significant role in this advocacy. Publications like Macaela Mackenzie's *Money, Power, Respect* (2023) explore the challenges women face in achieving gender equality in sports and highlight the progress made so far.

Global efforts, including international organizations and events, also advocate for gender equality, showcasing significant milestones and moments that promote equal opportunities for women.

Professional Opportunities

The growth of women's sports is opening up more professional opportunities for women in running. Increased visibility and popularity of women's sports translate into more career opportunities, from professional athletes to coaching, sponsorships, and media roles.

As women's sports gain more attention, there are better support structures for women athletes, including access to high-quality coaching, financial support through sponsorships, and increased media representation. These resources are crucial for women athletes to succeed professionally and achieve their full potential in the sport.

Efforts to champion women in running are reshaping the sport into a more inclusive and supportive community. These initiatives tackle various challenges, from boosting women's leadership roles to breaking down barriers to participation.

One key focus is on getting more women into leadership positions within running organizations. This not only gives female runners role models but also ensures their needs are considered in decision-making.

Advocates also work to tear down barriers that prevent women from joining in. This means addressing issues like safety concerns, lack of gear, or cultural barriers. By making running more accessible, more women can lace up their sneakers and hit the pavement.

However, it's not just about getting women in the door; it's about helping them thrive. That's why there are programs tailored to women's needs, like training and mentorship opportunities. These programs empower women to chase their running dreams with confidence.

Another vital aspect is challenging stereotypes and fostering a culture of respect. This means calling out discrimination and harassment and promoting body positivity. By creating a supportive environment, women feel valued and encouraged to push their limits.

In a nutshell, these efforts are transforming running into a sport where women of all backgrounds and abilities feel welcomed and empowered. By breaking down barriers, providing support, and promoting respect, the running community is becoming a place where every woman can thrive effortlessly.

A Call to Action for the Next Generation of Women Runners

Running is an amazing sport that offers so many opportunities and rewards. It's about pushing your limits, growing stronger, and connecting with others. As you lace up your shoes and head out, remember you are part of a long legacy of empowerment and excellence.

Running has a rich history of women who have broken barriers and set new standards. Think of Elaine Thompson-Herah, a sprinting superstar whose lightning speed has earned her countless medals and inspired a generation.

But Thompson-Herah is just one chapter in a book filled with trailblazers. From Wilma Rudolph, who dominated the track in the face of countless hurdles, to Kathrine Switzer, who ran marathons when women weren't even allowed, these women paved the way for us all.

Now, it's your turn. Strive for greatness, support your fellow runners, and inspire those who look up to you.

As you progress in your running journey, take the time to mentor younger runners. Share your experiences, offer guidance, and be a source of encouragement. Helping others enriches your running experience and contributes to their success.

The future of women's running is bright, and you are an important part of it. Don't run away from the challenges; get involved in your community, promote inclusivity, advocate for safety, fight for equality, and continue the legacy of those who came before you. By doing so, you will achieve your personal goals and inspire and empower the next generation of women runners.

Lessons From the Field

The stories and insights this book shares highlight several key lessons that must be a strong part of you. Every runner faces challenges, whether overcoming an injury, pushing through a tough race, or simply finding the motivation to get out the door each day. The stories in this book show that resilience is about pushing through difficulties, learning from setbacks, and coming back stronger. Embrace challenges as opportunities to grow, and remember that each obstacle you overcome builds your inner strength and determination.

Runners have each other's backs. Joining local running groups, going on group runs, and connecting with other runners can give you the support and sense of belonging you need. The stories in this book show us how communities can help us reach our goals and make running more fun. Get involved with your local running community, support others, and let them support you back.

Running isn't just about getting fit; it's about growing as a person. Setting goals and working hard to achieve them boosts our confidence and sense of accomplishment. The stories we've read show us how running can help us discover more about ourselves, improve our mental health, and better understand ourselves. Think about how running has helped you grow, and use that growth to keep pushing yourself forward.

As you approach the final pages of this book, you've traveled through the inspiring history and exciting future of women's running. You've met the brave pioneers who broke barriers and the innovative visionaries shaping the sport today.

Reflecting on this journey, you've seen the incredible resilience, determination, and passion that have driven women runners forward. Their stories remind us of the power of perseverance and the limitless potential within each of us.

Now, as we approach the end of our adventure, let's remember why we embarked on this journey: to celebrate the achievements of women runners, to ignite a fire of inspiration in our hearts, and to build a strong community of support for all women runners.

To everyone on this journey with us, now's the moment to dive deeper into the world of running. Whether you're a seasoned athlete or just dipping your toes, you'll find a supportive community here. So, tighten your shoelaces, tackle the hurdles, and let's keep shaping the tale of women running side by side.

Ahead lies a road full of opportunities and thrilling experiences. Let's leave our mark and ignite the passion in generations to come!

Bonus Chapter

I figured - I'll either pass out or I'll finish. —Jasmin Paris

Human beings have one common innate shortcoming: we tend to underestimate ourselves until we discover our superpowers, which go beyond mere brainpower. Throughout the majority of our existence, we hold steadfast to the notion that our brains wield ultimate authority. However, there come occasions when it—the brain—assumes a subordinate role, yielding to the impulses and intricacies of our deeper selves. Such occasions make you willing, ready, and capable of breaking limits, especially when you may be battling with a chronically doubtful subconscious as you seek the runners' crown.

While it's great to want to break limits and tackle whatever stumbling block exists in your running career, understanding the essence of incorporating different factors that would contribute to your great finishing will go a long way toward helping you achieve your long-term record-breaking goals. I like to think about these factors in three major categories.

- **Self-motivation:** The first step to developing self-motivation is to surround yourself with positive influences, inspirational stories, or books like the one you're reading now. Self-motivation also involves setting specific measurable, achievable, relevant, and time-bound (SMART) goals that will keep you focused and provide a clear direction toward your intended record-breaking achievements. Also, challenge negative thoughts with positive affirmations to build confidence and mental resilience during training and races.

- **Preparation:** A wise man once said that your preparation meets your success. So, you have to stay prepared by developing a training plan that incorporates different types of runs structured to improve speed, endurance, and overall fitness. Equally, you need to keep your body invigorated with the right nutrients to optimize performance and schedule adequate rest days and recovery practices to prevent or minimize injuries and ensure optimal fitness.

- **Teamwork:** Teamwork should be one factor you should never operate without. In all your endeavors, do not walk—or run—alone, as solo running is arguably less rewarding when you think long-term. You can get personalized guidance from a coach who will also guide you on some training plans and hold you accountable for achieving your goals. Training with a partner(s) can boost motivation and accountability and push you to perform better during workouts. Overall, you should have a supportive network of family, friends, or informal running groups that can provide encouragement and celebrate your achievements.

Remember that consistency and an integral approach toward your pursuit are key. So, by focusing on all three aspects—self-motivation, preparation, and teamwork—and undertaking minute actions that fall within these aspects, you'll be well on your way to smashing those records in no distant time.

About Women Breaking Records

The truth remains that it costs the best female sprinters we have today a lot to get to the level they are. Their wins are neither a product of one-time training undergone nor a single hurdle overcome; rather, they are a progressive collection of challenges well handled, which in turn builds resilience over time.

From the great female runners who fought for women's inclusivity to the ones who fought for maternity rights, the pioneers of the path paved the way for the present generation to have it easier. But is the present generation truly having an easier experience? If you ask me, I wouldn't say they are. There is no Yes or No answer to the question because evolution keeps bringing new challenges that either never existed or weren't recognized as such several years back. However, even as challenges abound, women have kept winning. It has almost become the norm to experience pride in accomplishment at different points in time, as women in running keep achieving great feats that are continuously serving as a fountain of inspiration for the next generation.

In the course of writing this book, my original intention was to conclude at this point, but a recent occasion shattered my plans beautifully and amazingly. Just as I, and perhaps the sporting world at large, assumed the narrative that achievements in women's sprinting had reached a plateau, an athlete known for her relentlessness exploded onto the scene, shattering expectations with a very blistering stride and creating yet another "first in history" record with her win. Events like this often show that anyone can be whatever they set their minds to be.

Not long ago, the 2024 Barkley Ultramarathon concluded. However, there was a highlight in this sports event as Jasmin Paris became the first woman to reach the gate—amid four male athletes. It is a beautiful reminder that the potential for greatness in this arena has only just begun to be tapped. While I am excited to share this mind-blowing win of Jasmine Paris with you, I'd love to prove to you first that she has always been a beast of an athlete. A little introspection into her eventful life would tell you exactly what I mean.

Who Is Jasmine Paris?

Jasmin Paris is a remarkable figure in the world of ultrarunning, whose accomplishments have captured the bewilderment of both the running community and the general public. Her journey from a background in hill running to becoming one of the world's most celebrated ultrarunners is nothing short of inspiring and empowering.

After her birth in Manchester in 1983, Paris had a normal, regular childhood, and as she grew older, she moved to Edinburgh, Scotland. By this time, Paris had developed a love for outdoor games. Growing up and surrounded by the pleasant landscapes of Scotland, she naturally gravitated towards outdoor activities, particularly running. However, her journey into the world of competitive running took shape when she joined Carnethy Hill Running Club, a renowned club known for its emphasis on hill running and fell running.

Jasmin Paris's Beginning in Hill Running

Hill running is also called mountain running, and it involves racing over rough terrain, most times at high altitudes. This presents unique challenges compared to road running or track running. The rugged terrain, unpredictable weather conditions, and steep ascents and descents make hill running a demanding yet interesting and adventurous sport. It requires not only physical strength and endurance but also mental resilience and navigation skills.

For Paris, hill running provided the perfect platform to showcase her talents and push her limits. She had been able to quickly establish herself as a formidable force in the hill running community, with numerous victories and podium finishes in prestigious races across Scotland and the UK over time. Her natural, relentless work ethic, as well as her athleticism and love for the sport, propelled her to the upper strata of hill running. However, it was her thrust into the world of ultramarathon that has truly cemented Jasmin's legacy in the world of endurance sports.

Jasmin Paris's Ultramarathon Career

In the simplest terms, an ultramarathon is any race that is longer than the marathon distance of 26.2 miles (42.2 kilometers). Ultramarathons can vary quite drastically in distance, though, and encompass anything from a single-day 50-K (31-mile) race to a multi-stage event spanning hundreds of kilometers. Unlike road marathons, which are usually confined to smooth, paved surfaces, ultramarathons often involve more challenging terrain—from soggy fells to sand dunes—and are designed to test both your physical endurance and mental toughness (Barraclough, 2023). Ultrarunning often presents a whole new set of challenges and demands on the body and mind. Ultramarathon or ultrarunning is one of the sports capable of testing the limits of human endurance and pushing runners to their breaking point.

Jasmin Paris's ultrarunning debut came in 2015 when she participated in the British Ultra Trail Championships and emerged the winner. This victory served as a springboard for her, leading her to an ultrarunning career and signaling her arrival as a force to be reckoned with in the ultradistance running community. With each race, she continued to defy expectations and shatter records, earning the respect and admiration of her peers and fans alike.

Again, at the 2019 Montane Spine Race, she made an epic performance that skyrocketed her status further up in the world of ultramarathons. Also known as "Britain's most brutal race," the Montane Spine Race is an arduous 268-mile ultramarathon along the entire length of the Pennine Way, a long-distance footpath in England. The race cuts across some of the most rugged and remote terrain in the UK, including bogs, moors, and steep mountain passes, making it a true test of endurance.

What made Jasmin Paris's victory at the 2019 Montane Spine Race stand out was not just her win but the manner in which she achieved it. Not only did she become the first woman to win the race outright, but she also set a new course record, completing the daunting course in an unbelievable 83 hours, 12 minutes, and 23 seconds. What was even more incredible was that she accomplished this feat while expressing breast milk for her baby daughter, Rowan, during breaks along the route.

Balancing biological demands and sporting expectations has continued to make women in sports uniquely strong and resilient. Juggling the demands of motherhood with the rigors of ultrarunning is no small feat, yet Jasmin Paris managed to do so with grace and determination. Her ability to balance her roles as a mother, wife, and elite athlete is proof of her strength of character and unrelenting dedication to her passions. In interviews, she has spoken candidly about the challenges of being a competitive athlete and a parent, frankly acknowledging the struggles, sacrifices, and compromises that come with both roles.

In addition to her accomplishments on the track, Jasmin Paris is also a talented and accomplished scientific scholar. She holds a PhD in veterinary science from the University of Edinburgh and works as a researcher at the Roslin Institute, where she studies infectious diseases in livestock. Her balance in her pursuits has complemented her athletic endeavors, giving a unique insight and in-depth understanding of her drive.

Jasmine Paris's Latest Big Win

Jasmine hadn't stopped when the world thought she did; she was probably only strategizing for something bigger. Having imprinted her name in the sand of marathon records for over a decade, one would think that the 40-year-old would gradually slow down, but she has proven once more that she is very much around and fit. In the 2024 Barkley Ultramarathon, Jasmin emerged as the first woman finisher amid four male finishers. She had attempted and succeeded at breaking the broken records that had been long-standing for a few years.

Two unique things happened during the just concluded Barkley Ultramarathon: an all-time high number of finishers and the first female finisher were recorded. As against the standing record of three finishers, all men, in the 2012 Barkley Ultramarathon, this year saw a new milestone of five finishers, of which there was one woman. Of the two records, the one that stood out for many, as you can rightly guess, was Jasmine's win. She achieved a milestone many have mentally ruled out that women would ever achieve: the almighty, strength-testing Barkley.

As explicitly described by (Pearson & Bozon, 2024), the marathon course consists of 5 roughly 20-mile loops in the woods and requires runners to rip pages from books on the course to prove they've followed the unmarked route. There are approximately 13,000 feet of vertical elevation gain per loop, which amounts to a total elevation gain of 65,616 feet—more than twice the height of Mount Everest—over the 100-mile course. Each loop must be completed in 12 hours to even attempt the full course, with the overall cut-off time being 60 hours.

Key Insight From Jasmin Paris's Victory

Afterward, Jasmin Paris shared her post-marathon experience and recounted her final, gutsy, triumphant push up the Big Cove campground road to the Frozen Headgate in her bid to finish under 60 hours and make history for every woman in running. In the midst of swollen legs, inflamed tendons, and all, Paris was happy to clutch onto and take pride in her win happily. Finishing within the last 120 seconds of the 60-hour time frame was also a scintillating experience, as every lover of resilience from all over the world wished Jasmin nothing but success. The bitter-sweet experience that comes with embarking on a tasking but successful course is evident in her story and is truly empowering, especially to runners like you who earnestly desire to break records.

All it implies is that, regardless of the effort you may have put in or be willing to put in to achieve that great breakthrough, you do not have to overthink it. Your result will supersede your investment because, in the end, it would all be worth it—the several hours of training, the sacrifices, the discomfort. They all count as a cardinal part of your success story.

Conclusion

Imagine you're standing at the starting line of a race, eager to take off. But just like a car sputters without fuel or struggles to respond without electricity, you might find yourself hesitant to push forward if you haven't built your propelling force through the right motivation, structure, and support. These are the sparks that ignite your running journey and propel you towards your goals. Think of motivation as the fuel in your tank. It's the fire that gets you excited to lace up your running shoes and hit the track. A well-drilled mind, stocked with positive thoughts and clear goals, keeps that fire burning bright and never needs to die down.

Structure, on the other hand, is your roadmap. It guides you through your training, ensuring you build endurance and strength at a healthy pace. Without a structured plan, you might end up running in circles instead of a straight line—or you might be stuck, frustrated, and unsure of the next step to take.

Similarly, a supportive network is your cheering section. It's the high-fives from friends, the encouraging words from family, and the camaraderie of your fellow runners who understand the challenges and triumphs of this journey. Having a support system by your side can make all the difference, especially when motivation seems to take a dip or the road gets tougher.

So, as you embark on your running adventure, remember to fuel your passion, navigate with a plan, and surround yourself with a supportive crew. With these elements in place, you'll be well on your way to achieving your running goals and experiencing the incredible joy that comes with this amazing sport. The information shared in this book not only gives you an understanding of the concept of drawing motivation from the experiences of women in running but also provides scenarios that give a clear perspective of reality. This book takes pride in its comprehensive yet intimate exploration of women's long-distance running, combining historical insights, scientific understanding, as well as personal efforts, all aimed to achieve one goal—inspire you, then advise you.

We did not halt at merely celebrating the encouraging achievements of these great women but also delved deep into the physiological, psychological, and societal aspects specific to women runners. This way, both inspiration and practical advice were gained. This book looks back on the early days when women first started being included in running. It shares stories that show what can be possible and achievable, even in a world where succeeding is tough.

As much as it is clear that the stories are not mere charades aimed to sing praises of women, it is fair to state that with the right mindset, stories in this book can easily serve as a compass, directing and guiding your strides as you embark on a journey of history-making. The personal narratives are nothing but a reservoir of strength, motivation, fortitude, and every other thing it takes to not only break records but to stay fulfilled while doing so.

Key Takeaways

If you read to this point in this book, it is assumed that you have any of these key things to hold onto:

- Running is beyond a sport and will always require support from yourself and others.

- Understanding your body as a woman and as a human helps you to navigate running challenges with more ease.

- Being a woman does not keep you at any running disadvantage.

- Do not joke around with joining running communities and networks. They will always turn out to be your bearing at low moments.

- Every record breaker has a backstory for everyone to learn from and be inspired by.

- You, too, can break a record. But while at it, don't be too hard on yourself.

Women in running often face discouragement and lack of support from family, friends, or society. This is more dominant in cultures where women's sports are not widely accepted or encouraged. They struggle with internalized beliefs about their physical capabilities or face logistic barriers like finding time for training or traveling certain distances for reinforcements due to domestic commitments. Also, female runners often need guidance on how to navigate health issues, especially concerning running. This includes understanding the impact of hormones on performance, preventing injuries, and addressing concerns around pregnancy and running postpartum.

Many female runners feel that the running community and resources often overlook the specific challenges and needs they face, such as training around menstrual cycles, dealing with safety concerns, and balancing running with family or career obligations. This book has attempted to identify and proffer solutions to these aforementioned challenges while telling legendary stories to provide some inspiration.

Final Words

Dear ambitious running enthusiast like myself,

It is your turn to embrace the path ahead with the strength and spirit of those who ran before you.

It's your time to set the pace, break barriers, and inspire the next stride in the endless and exhilarating race of running.

It has reached a stage where you move from reading about broken records to breaking records yourself that the universe will read about.

Dear superwoman,

Would you rather the negative conceptions about women's willpower derail your journey and weaken your core?

Would you rather choose to start building now or postpone the course for an unending later?

Would you not start seeking to draw some strength, stay on your guard, and face this running fight?

Remember that procrastination is a lazy man's apology, and a resilient sportswoman is known to be unapologetic and excuse-free.

Day one or One day? It is all in your legs now. Go push the pace and finish strong!

Before I bid my final goodbye, I would be glad to hear how this book has impacted you, especially as a young woman interested in sports.

How has the information herein shaped your mindset?

In what ways have the stories inspired you?

I hope that whatever benefit you get from this book is something you would gladly put into practice.

I hope that you will recommend this book to that young athletic woman you know because, just like you, she deserves to be inspired, too.

See you at the top!

Sarah Russell's Unbridled Resilience : Women in Running

Review Request Page

Thank you so much for reading *Unbridled Resilience: Women in Running*. I hope these stories of courage, determination, and passion have inspired you, just as they have inspired me.

Now that you've reached the finish line of this book, I have one small favor to ask—would you consider leaving a review?

Your thoughts and feedback not only mean the world to me, but they also help other readers discover these powerful stories of women who continue to push boundaries in the running world. A quick review can make a huge impact, helping more people find inspiration and strength in the pages of this book.

Sharing your experience could help:

- One more woman find motivation to lace up her running shoes.
- One more reader discover the unstoppable spirit inside themselves.
- One more dreamer realize they, too, can go the distance.

If you'd like to support this mission, you can leave a review by simply scanning the QR code below:

Thank you for being part of this incredible journey. Your words have the power to inspire others—just like the amazing women in this book.

With gratitude,
Sarah Russell

References

Adidas. (2023, March 10). *New Adidas study finds that 92% of women are concerned for their safety when they go for a run.* Adidas News Site. https://news.adidas.com/running/new-adidas-study-finds-92--of-women-are-concerned-for-their-safety-when-they-go-for-a-run/s/c318f69e-7575-4ced-bbf3-9db6d2ab1642##endref[1%20to%207]

Andrews, M. (2022, November 16). *What is ultra running? Ultramarathons, explained.* Marathon Handbook. https://marathonhandbook.com/what-is-ultra-running/

Barraclough, A. (2023, July 10). Going beyond 26.2 miles: the ultimate guide to ultramarathon training. Runner's World. https://www.runnersworld.com/uk/training/ultra/a44426743/ultra-marathon/

Burdick, A. (2013, September 5). *Getting "chicked" - A history of women's running.* Runners Connect. https://runnersconnect.net/women-runners-then-and-now/

Caesar, E. (2015, June 30). What was the secret of Paula Radcliffe's exceptional London Marathon? *The Guardian.* https://www.theguardian.com/lifeandstyle/the-running-blog/2015/jun/30/secret-paula-radcliffe-2003-london-marathon

Carter, K. (2023, January 10). *How your menstrual cycle affects your running – and how to adapt.* Runner's World. https://www.runnersworld.com/uk/health/a42404501/exercise-menstrual-cycle/

Darvin, L. (2023, October 31). Media coverage for women's sports has nearly tripled in five years, according to new research. *Forbes.* https://www.forbes.com/sites/lindseyedarvin/2023/10/31/media-coverage-for-womens-sports-has-nearly-tripled-in-five-years-according-to-new-research/

DeCesaris, L. (2023, January 31). *How different exercises affect women's hormones.* Rupa Health. https://www.rupahealth.com/post/exercise-affects-on-womens-hormones

Ellis, B. (2023, August 22). *Courtney Dauwalter's training, workouts and diet.* RunBryanRun. https://runbryanrun.com/courtney-dauwalters-training-workouts-and-diet/

Foster, M. (2023, April 29). Courtney Dauwalter: The fun-fueled ultra-marathon star defying science. *CNN.* https://edition.cnn.com/2023/04/29/sport/courtney-dauwalter-ultramarathon-spt-intl/index.html

Gabe Grunewald. (n.d.). Brave like Gabe. https://www.bravelikegabe.org/about

Goal Five. (2022, February 23). *History of gender inequality in sports: Definitive guide.* Goal Five.

https://goalfive.com/blogs/news/history-of-gender-inequality-in-sports

Greally, F. (2004, June 1). *Paula Radcliffe's journey from disappointing fourth to dominant first*. Runner's World. https://www.runnersworld.com/advanced/a20842101 /paula-radcliffes-journey-from-disappointing-fourth-to-dominant-first/

Grete Waitz: A life in the lead. (n.d.) NYRR. https://www.nyrr.org/about/hall-of-fame/grete-waitz

International Olympic Committee. (n.d.). *Tirunesh DIBABA*. International Olympic Committee. https://olympics.com/en/athletes/tirunesh-dibaba

Jennings, M. (2023, January 10). The added challenges of being a woman runner. *The Irish Times*. https://www.irishtimes.com/health/your-fitness/2023/01/10/the-added-challenges-of-being-a-woman-runner/

Joan Benoit Samuelson | 1984 Olympics, family, age, & books. (2024, May 13). Encyclopedia Britannica. https://www.britannica.com/biography/Joan-Benoit-Samuelson

Kessel, A. (2013, April, 13). Paula Radcliffe recalls her "impossible" London marathon record run. *The Guardian*. https://www.theguardian.com/sport/2013/apr/20/paula-radcliffe-london-marathon-record

Leigey, D., Irrgang, J., Francis, K., Cohen, P., & Wright, V. (2009). Participation in high-impact sports predicts bone mineral density in senior Olympic athletes. *Sports Health: A Multidisciplinary Approach, 1*(6), 508–513. https://doi.org/10.1177/1941738109347979

L'Heveder, A., Chan, M., Mitra, A., Kasaven, L., Saso, S., Prior, T., Pollock, N., Dooley, M., Joash, K., & Jones, B. P. (2022). Sports obstetrics: Implications of pregnancy in elite sportswomen, a narrative Review. *Journal of Clinical Medicine, 11*(17), 4977. https://doi.org/10.3390/jcm11174977

Louw, M. (2023, February 17). *How the menopause affects a runner's body.* Sports Injury Physio. https://www.sports-injury-physio.com/post/how-the-menopause-affects-a-runner-s-body

Mackay, D. (2002, July 27). Masai making up for a late start with a fast finish. *The Guardian.* https://www.theguardian.com/sport/2002/jul/27/commonwealthgames2002.commonwealthgames2

Metzler, B. (2023, September 8). Leadville's Courtney Dauwalter wins unprecedented "triple crown" of ultrarunning. *The Colorado Sun.* https://coloradosun.com/2023/09/08/courtney-dauwalter-ultrarunning-triple-crown/

Mikhail, A. (2024, July 16). Track star and entrepreneur Allyson Felix will launch the Olympic Village's first nursery: 'The systems aren't in place for mothers whatsoever'. Fortune Well.

https://fortune.com/well/2024/07/16/allyson-felix-olympic-village-nursery-mothers/

Narin, S., & Ives, M. (2023, May 25). *This runner finished last, but her perseverance won over a nation. The New York Times.* https://www.nytimes.com/2023/05/25/sports/bou-samnang-cambodian-runner-rain.html

Never done breaking barriers: Joan Benoit Samuelson's legacy. (n.d.). Nike. https://www.nike.com/ph/a/never-done-breaking-barriers-joan-benoit-samuelsons-legacy

Parker, T. (2023, January 31). *African legend: Tirunesh Dibaba.* Selamta. https://selamta.ethiopianairlines.com/people/african-legend-tirunesh-dibaba/

Parren, A. (2023, December 20). *Does running affect our hormones?* Women's Running. https://www.womensrunning.co.uk/health/running-and-hormones/

Pearson, R., & Bozon, J. (2024, March 23). *Five runners — including the first woman ever — complete the 2024 Barkley Marathons.* Runner's World. https://www.runnersworld.com/uk/training/motivation/a43322798/barkley-marathons/

Rizzo, N. (2021, December 20). *What women runners need to know about bone health.* Women's Running. https://www.womensrunning.com/health/what-women-runners-need-to-know-about-bone-health/

Sayer, A., & Turbett, J. (2023, August 8). *These 11 benefits of running are actually backed by science.* The Manual.

https://www.themanual.com/fitness/benefits-of-running/

Schwartz, K. (2023, October 31). *Why you should join a running club*. Fleet Feet. https://www.fleetfeet.com/blog/why-you-should-join-a-running-club

Slaney, Mary Decker (1958—). (2024, June 14). Encyclopedia.com. https://www.encyclopedia.com/women/encyclopedias-almanacs-transcripts-and-maps/slaney-mary-decker-1958

Snider-McGrath, B. (2020, April 30). Shalane Flanagan, new mom. *Canadian Running Magazine*. https://runningmagazine.ca/the-scene/shalane-flanagan-new-mom/

Tirunesh Dibaba. (n.d.) Olympedia. https://www.olympedia.org/athletes/104973

Walsh, G. (2023, May 15). How running changed my life: "I have built my body from nothing." *Woman and Home Magazine*. https://www.womanandhome.com/health-wellbeing/how-running-changed-my-life/

Warner, L. (2022, May 12). *The athlete's guide to menopause*. Outside Online. https://www.outsideonline.com/health/training-performance/menopause-exercise-tips/

Wendy, W. (n.d.). *A brief history of women's running*. Custom Performance. https://www.nycustompt.com/a-brief-history-of-women-running/

What to know about running to lose weight. (2024, February 18). WebMD. https://www.webmd.com/fitness-exercise/running-to-lose-weight

Made in United States
North Haven, CT
27 February 2025

66318443R00093